Praise for

Relaxing into the process of writing is hardly a common approach to composition. But given most students' negative attitudes toward writing and the alarming reports of growing teenage depression and anxiety, it could just be the shift teachers need to make. Rather than forcing students to write, Dan Tricarico suggests that we invite students to write for authentic purposes and actual audiences. Compliance rarely fosters creativity.

—**Carol Jago,** associate director of the California Reading and Literature Project at UCLA and author of *The Book in Question: Why and How Reading Is in Crisis*

What sets this book apart from other writing manuals is the explicit understanding that writing is a social and emotional process. Tricarico demonstrates through humorous guidance, relevant examples, and personal stories that the writing process is a personal journey that extends knowledge of ourselves and others. In this book, readers and writers will focus on self-awareness, persistence, goal-setting, mindfulness, and developing a growth mindset. Tricarico inspires readers of all ages to realize that they, too, can be writers.

—**Dr. Krista Leh,** owner and CEO of Resonance Educational Consulting

Even as a writer and meditation practitioner, I'm so grateful for all the new wisdom, reflection, inspiration, and practice my friend Dan Tricarico shares in this exquisite book. Whether you are a writer, a teacher, or any kind of creative, you'll find pearls of wisdom sprinkled throughout this warmly supportive and down-to-earth book!

—**Dr. Christopher Willard,** author of *Growing Up Mindful: Essential Practices to Help Children, Teens, and Families Find Balance, Calm, and Resilience*

In *Write Here and Now*, Dan Tricarico helps students and teachers create a more calm, tranquil, and relaxed environment. Tricarico's solid pedagogy, fun and practical lessons, gentle sense of humor, and decades of experience as a writing teacher not only offer profound opportunities for creativity but also create an unusual chance for both teacher and student to explore and, as it turns out, better understand their world through words. If you're a writer—on either side of the desk—you need this book.

—**Dr. Deborah E. Louis,** owner and CEO of the Jane Schaffer Academic Writing Program®

Also by Dan Tricarico

The Zen Teacher

Creating Focus, Simplicity, and Tranquility in the Classroom

Teachers have incredible power to influence—even improve—the future. In *The Zen Teacher*, educator, blogger, and speaker Dan Tricarico provides practical, easy-to-use techniques to help teachers be their best—unrushed and fully focused—so they can maximize their performance and improve their quality of life. In this introductory guide, Dan Tricarico explains what it means to develop a Zen practice—something that has nothing to do with religion and everything to do with your ability to thrive in the classroom.

Sanctuaries

Self-Care Secrets for Stressed-Out Teachers

Living in a constant state of "crazy-busy" doesn't help anyone, least of all you. To be at your best for others, you must first be your own best self, which requires slowing down and becoming aware of—and tending to—your own needs. The simple, practical, and actionable steps Dan Tricarico (author of *The Zen Teacher*) shares in this guide will empower you to create a sanctuary plan that allows you to experience more peace and less stress—starting today. If *The Zen Teacher* reminds you to take care of yourself, *Sanctuaries* shows you how.

Write Here and Now

Dan Tricarico

Write
Here and Now

The Mindful Writing Teacher's
Guide to Finding the
Zen in Their Pen

Write Here and Now: The Mindful Writing Teacher's Guide to Finding the Zen in Their Pen
© 2022 Dan Tricarico

All rights reserved. No part of this publication may be reproduced in any form or by any electronic or mechanical means, including information storage and retrieval systems, without permission in writing by the publisher, except by a reviewer who may quote brief passages in a review. For information regarding permission, contact the publisher at books@daveburgessconsulting.com.

> This book is available at special discounts when purchased in quantity for educational purposes or for use as premiums, promotions, or fundraisers. For inquiries and details, contact the publisher at books@daveburgessconsulting.com.

Published by Dave Burgess Consulting, Inc.
San Diego, CA
DaveBurgessConsulting.com

Library of Congress Control Number: 2022946569
Paperback ISBN: 978-1-956306-39-2
Ebook ISBN: 978-1-956306-40-8

Cover and interior design by Liz Schreiter
Edited and produced by Reading List Editorial
ReadingListEditorial.com

To Christine Pestolis McDuff

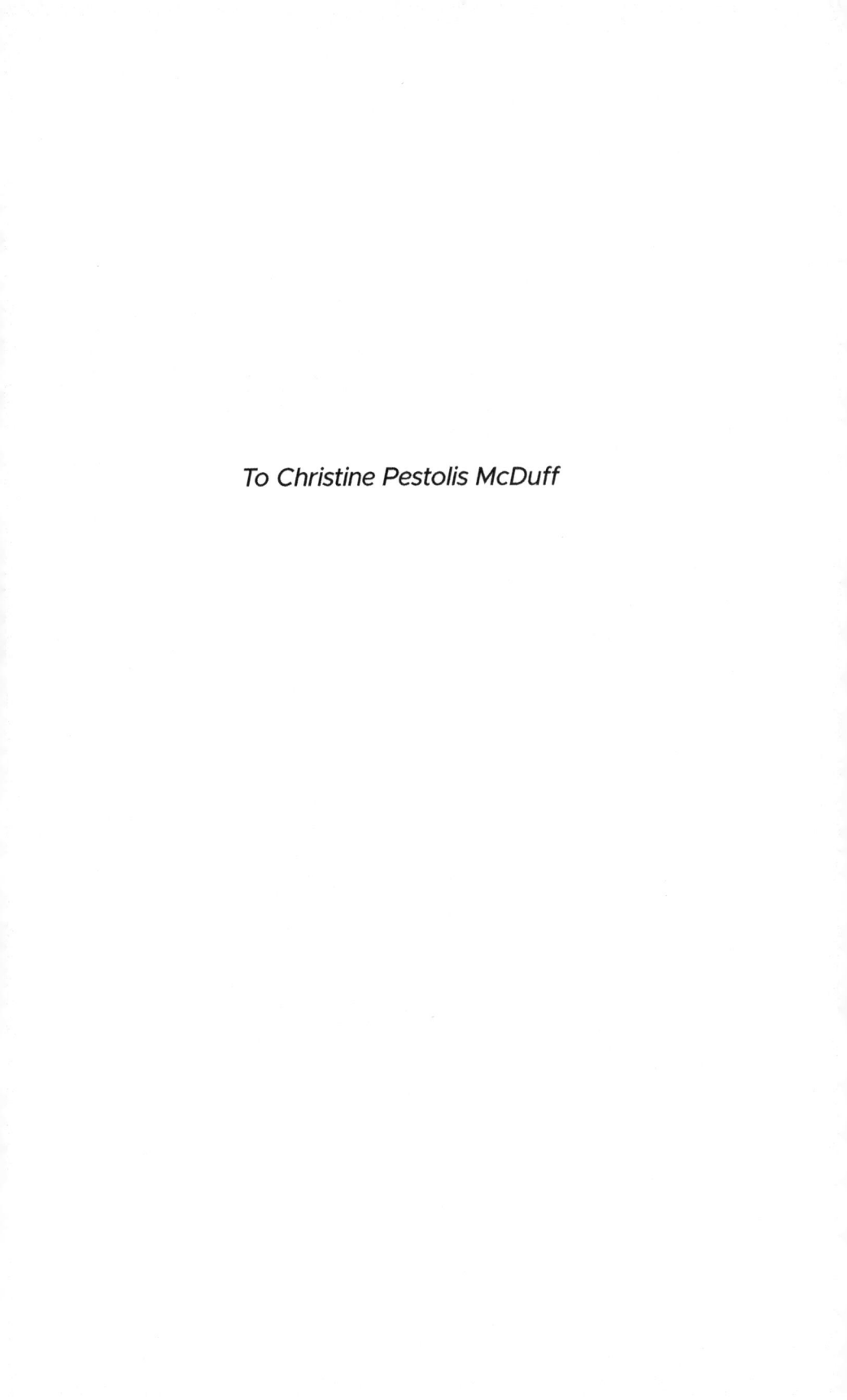

Contents

Introduction 1

Guiding Principles

Chapter 1: Why Write? 9
Chapter 2: Writing Is a Path 14

Planning

Chapter 3: Thinking. 20
Chapter 4: Woolgathering 23
Chapter 5: Nonjudgment 27
Chapter 6: The Ugly Prewrite 30
Chapter 7: Prewriting. 33

Drafting

Chapter 8: Beginner's Mind 42
Chapter 9: Five Hundred Words 47
Chapter 10: Wind Sprints 53
Chapter 11: Journaling as Meditation 58
Chapter 12: BIC. 66
Chapter 13: Rituals 69
Chapter 14: Paying Attention 75
Chapter 15: White Space 80

Blank Pages and Disappointments

Chapter 16: Lovingkindness 86
Chapter 17: Writer's Block 91
Chapter 18: Intuition 102
Chapter 19: Writing Is a Continuum 105

Revision

Chapter 20: Peer Response 114
Chapter 21: Revision 118
Chapter 22: Precision. 123
Chapter 23: Clarity 127
Chapter 24: Words to Avoid. 134
Chapter 25: Set It Aside 138

Finishing

Chapter 26: Being Done 143
Chapter 27: Celebrate the Victories. 145
Chapter 28: Detachment. 149
Chapter 29: Multiple Drafts 154
Chapter 30: Presentation 158
Chapter 31: Gestation 163
Conclusion: Start a New Path 170

About the Author. 173
References 175
Acknowledgments 178
More from Dave Burgess Consulting, Inc. 180

> A word after a word after a word is power.
>
> —Margaret Atwood

Introduction

In the early years of my writing practice, I never realized how mindful it could be to simply put words to paper. Yet mindfulness was always there, percolating just below the surface. With poetry, there was the attention to detail. With journalism, there was focusing on the current moment. With fiction, there was the empathy and compassion associated with living among other human beings, not to mention the exploration of the fundamental truths of life. Though I didn't see it, mindfulness was everywhere in the writing process. Looking back, I now must admit that writing has always been one of the most mindful experiences of my life.

There are, I suppose, worse ways to stay grounded.

Simply put, mindfulness is the practice of being present and living in the current moment, free from distraction and judgment. Pursuing writing with an eye toward mindfulness can make putting pen to paper or fingers to keyboard a much easier activity, as well as a more profound experience. I've learned that writing poetry, for example, is its own form of mindfulness. Poetry, all by itself, taught me how to be in the present moment, how to notice details, and how to capture specific events by focusing on what is, without judgment. It's a lovely way to live.

I have been a writer my entire life. In my classroom is a footlocker that contains just about everything I've ever written from the time I was eight or nine: stacks of song lyrics, thousands of poems, dozens of short stories and flash fiction pieces, three sitcom episodes, a handful of essays and articles, two movie screenplays, one two-act stage play, and three unpublished novels.

Furthermore, I have a background in journalism and freelance writing. I've been a reporter and editor for a number of newspapers (before newspapers went the way of the dinosaurs, minus the meteor), and I've had many articles and dozens of poems printed both in print and online. I am also the author of three published nonfiction books, including my signature tome, *The Zen Teacher: Creating Focus, Simplicity, and Tranquility in the Classroom*.

But as much as I love writing, at some point in my teaching career, I had to accept that not all of my students enjoyed it as much as I did. I also had to accept that even my colleagues in English departments across the world didn't enjoy writing as much as I did. In fact, I was shocked to learn that many do not do it at all.

I've always found that curious. And heartbreaking.

Imagine you are seeking violin lessons for your child. You find a renowned teacher who is well-versed in the ways of stringed instruments. The teacher's rate is reasonable, and they are clearly qualified. You're interested in hiring this person, but then you ask this highly reputable, well-credentialed prospective violin teacher to play something.

"Oh, I don't *play* the violin," the violin teacher says. "I just teach others."

At that point, you'd probably be in the market for another violin teacher.

Similarly, the problem with most writing teachers is that they simply don't do it themselves. If you are going to teach something as deeply and thoughtfully as possible, it seems to me that you should also be a practitioner.

This book is going to give you strategies, approaches, and tools you can use in the classroom to improve your writing instruction through the lens of mindfulness, but it will also show you how—and why—to improve your own writing practice.

I will talk about relaxing into the process, writing in the moment, and the benefits of meditating and reflecting on processes and strategies.

I will talk about noticing and observing the world around you—and let's face it, observation is really one of the writer's greatest superpowers.

Essentially, I will teach you how to use mindfulness to improve your writing and how to share that knowledge with your students.

Write Here and Now: The Mindful Writing Teacher's Guide to Finding the Zen in Their Pen is intended to give you some unconventional, and hopefully inspiring, ideas on how to increase the writer's joy when putting words to paper. The book is designed to help writers generate ideas, compose in the heat of the moment, revise and polish to improve each piece, and prepare a proper final draft. But that's not all. It is also my hope that this book will help you figure out what to do when you're uninspired, when the words won't come, or when you're slogging through a tough piece and aren't sure which keys to tap.

I want you to discover a little bit of the magic that can happen with writing if you are brave enough to go for it.

After sharing a few philosophical ideas in the section called "Guiding Principles," I've loosely structured this book around the five basic steps in the writing process. Each of these steps is a critical element in creating a piece of writing that you and your students can be proud of.

Here are those steps:

1. Planning
2. Drafting
3. Editing
4. Revision
5. Final Draft (Finishing)

Let's break them down.

1. **Planning.** This is where you plan, structure, and organize ideas before committing first words to paper.
2. **Drafting.** The rough draft is where you get down all your ideas and are consumed by the heat of composition. You are not immediately concerned with spelling, grammar, and punctuation. You're just getting it down.
3. **Editing.** Once you have a workable rough draft, it is critical to get another pair of eyes on it. Show your work to someone else. Get a peer response. Do a self-evaluation. Confront your writer's block. (I mean, if there was such a thing. More on that later.)
4. **Revision.** This is the step where you do whatever it takes to make your writing better, including repeating the editing and revision process as many times as necessary to put forward your best work. As I tell my students, "One draft is never enough. Multiple drafts is the norm."
5. **Final Draft (Finishing).** This is where your piece of writing puts on its tie and dress shoes and goes to work. This is where you type a nice, neat, presentable, professional version to submit to either a teacher or a publisher. It's also where you decide when you're finished and look ahead to what's next.

I have structured this book around these five elements because following the steps of the writing process makes you a mindful writer. This approach allows you to be conscious of the process, practice a set ritual, and envision writing as a journey with certain signposts instead of just an unstructured free-for-all with your pen or keyboard. And to get us started, in the first part of the book, I've laid out a few ideas on the philosophy of mindful writing.

One final note: Throughout the book you will see short interludes called "Danny's Writing Diary." These stories have been drawn from my own writing past—everything from a poem I wrote about one of my first crushes to the joy of my first published poem to watching the publishing success of one of my own students. I thought these would give you some insight into my writing journey over the years. These little vignettes are not related to the sections in the book; however, since they are presented chronologically, I hope they will give you an historical overview of my journey as a writer, including some of the highs and lows, tears and laughter that have come with having a writing practice of my own.

I hope you enjoy them.

Guiding Principles

CHAPTER 1

Why Write?

You know those writers who say they've been writing ever since they could hold a pencil? That's me. I've been writing for as long as I can remember, and if I go too long without doing it, I get cranky. I feel off. If more than a few days go by and I haven't taken up a pen or keyboard to jot down some thoughts or write a poem or work on a chapter in a new book, a profound restlessness creeps in.

Compulsive writers are only slightly less irksome than those folks who overshare about their commitment to Crossfit or fill up their Instagrams with half-marathon circuits or blog ceaselessly about the benefits of veganism. Much like the weight lifting, running, and tofu crowd, writers feel that our particular obsession—pushing nouns against verbs—makes us special and unique in some way.

But there's a reason we feel that way: We know a secret. We know that writing is a beautiful opportunity to explore how we feel and what we think. It's a chance to crystalize our thoughts and ideas so that we know how to move forward. It's a way of making sense of, and giving order to, the world. Clearly and effectively expressing what we think and feel in words is one of the most important skills we possess. And that's why, at least for me, writing is an obsession, a compulsion, an illness.

But now think about our public and private schools. We do not *ask* our students to write, nor do we even *allow* our students to write. The brutal truth is that we *force* our students to write. We tell them that it's good for them, as if it's castor oil for the mind or broccoli for the soul. Of course it *is* good for them, but let's be honest: most of them don't want to do it. And why would they? Tell the truth: When was the last time you wrote a multi-paragraph essay on *A Midsummer Night's Dream* or an argumentative piece discussing whether or not the latest Malcolm Gladwell article was sufficiently supported with effective evidence?

Come to think of it, when was the last time you wrote anything purely for your own enjoyment?

Did you jot down a poem about last night's sunset?

Doubtful.

Did you write a piece of flash fiction on your last summer break?

Hardly.

Did you crank out an episode review for your blog while bingeing *Game of Thrones*?

Definitely not.

You may be a teacher. Hell, you may even be an English teacher. But the odds are good that the last thing you wrote was probably that letter you stuff in your Christmas card saying that Evan just won the fifth-grade science fair and Jessica just got accepted to Pepperdine.

Of course, I kid.

I don't kid about the content—that probably *is* the last thing you wrote. I kid that it isn't okay. A warm and friendly Christmas letter is a wonderful thing and a lovely way to share your life with loved ones, and so why not?

But if we know that having our students write is important, why don't *we* do it more?

Why aren't we modeling it?

A question for the ages.

Writing (and literacy in general) should most certainly be a cross-curricular skill. In other words, students should be writing in every single class. That may just be my prejudice, but I don't think so. Research backs it up.

There are excellent writing teachers out there who may be even more fabulous editors, but I can't help but wonder how much better their students' writing skills would be if those teachers came into the classroom and said, "Wow! I was struggling with this piece last night, and I just couldn't get it to work. But I've been there before, and I know I'll figure it out. Just gotta keep writing."

Writing takes time. It takes focus and concentration, two qualities that are sadly in short supply in our current culture and in our current time, especially in the modern American classroom (standardized testing, anyone?).

So those folks who say they want to write something say things like, "Oh, I'd love to write, but I just don't have the time." The truth is, I don't either. Sometimes I get up woefully early. Sometimes I stay up late. Sometimes I write on my lunch period. I do what it takes. And it may require sacrifice. I don't watch as much television as the average person. At times, I've been a little too tired and grumpy with my family. I never work out. Okay, even if I never had the desire to write a single word, I'd probably never step foot in a gym, but you get my point. All of us have activities in our daily schedules, both critical and superfluous, necessary and indulgent, that we could—if we wanted to—streamline or eliminate in order to make time to write.

Ultimately, writing is a choice.

Knowing I had a desire to write, I adjusted a few small things in my schedule, and suddenly, I discovered thirty minutes, three times a week, and that's how this book was written. If you asked me straight out, I would say that I don't have time to write. But as I tell people, "Books don't write themselves." No one really has time to write. But I've written nine books with "no time to write," five of which have been published. If you want to do something, you find a way.

For students, though, it's not a matter of time. It's often a matter of motivation or investment. They often think: "Why write at all? What's in it for me?"

I can't tell anybody why *they* should write, but I can tell you why *I* write.

I write:

- to explore my feelings (journal, blog)
- to figure out what I think (journal, blog)
- to capture a moment (usually poetry)
- to *be* in the moment (poetry)
- to share my thoughts (blog)
- to tell a story (fiction)
- to brainstorm about my writing, life, and Zen Teacher stuff (my bullet journal)
- simply for fun (poetry, blog, fiction)
- to try to make sense of the world (all of the above).

I also write because, as I said at the beginning of this chapter, it relaxes me. Along with actual therapy, it's my therapy. Right this minute, for example, it's 7:30 a.m., and I am sitting in my classroom, sipping hot coffee as I type, listening to Billie Holiday on the boombox as a soft rain falls outside my classroom windows. It's absolute bliss. I am at peace and the world is right. As a bonus, I'm creating.

Even for this writer, though, it is hard to articulate in words how grateful I am that this nearly thirty-minute writing session will be one of the perfect moments of my day. But it will be.

Almost always, writing helps me understand what's going on.
It brings me a sense of inner peace and order.
And that's always worth half an hour of my day.

CHAPTER 2

Writing Is a Path

Where are you going?

Such a simple question. Yet in our creative endeavors, there can be so many different, confusing, and even contradictory answers that it's sometimes difficult to find our direction.

In writing, where you are going depends on many factors: your background, your desires, your skill level and experience, your obsessions, sometimes even your surroundings. Each has an impact on the path you will follow as a writer.

I come from a journalism background, for example. I wrote for my high school and college newspapers and spent many years getting paid little bits of money doing freelance work here and there. I composed short restaurant profiles for a local website; I wrote about music for a website dedicated to music and pop culture; I even spent a year as a columnist for *Scribophile*, an online community for writers. Working as a journalist, I learned a great deal about consistency, discipline, and the difference between objectivity and subjectivity. But mainly, I learned to see writing as both an art *and* a craft. What that means is that while inspiration is nice, my editors didn't care one whit if I was inspired or not. If my piece wasn't on their desks by the deadline, there'd be hell to pay.

Put another way: imagine that you build cabinets for a living, and you meet with a client and say, "I know I promised I'd have those kitchen cabinets installed by Friday, but I'm sorry; I just wasn't *feeling* it."

That wouldn't really fly, would it?

In order to get your work done, then, it helps to think of writing as a craft. Same as knitting, playing guitar, candle-making, or sleight-of-hand card tricks. "Write a little every day," Isak Dinesen once said, "without hope and without despair." Writing, as we will discuss later, is a continuum and, like any acquired skill, requires consistency and discipline. And in the end, the level of consistency you deploy and the structure of your discipline helps determine your path.

If you decide you're going to make writing a consistent part of your life, then writing becomes part of your path. It becomes part of what you're doing and where you're going. But finding your way on the path of writing is not always easy or straightforward.

Sometimes it can be downright circuitous.

As the Zen saying goes, "The goal is the path."

I may have started out in journalism, but more than anything, I wanted to write fiction. I either wanted to write poems and stories and novels that students would read in their classrooms centuries from now, or I wanted to be famous and make a ton of dough in my own lifetime by becoming the next Stephen King, Nora Roberts, Danielle Steele, James Patterson, Nicholas Sparks, or that lady who wrote *Twilight* (okay, maybe not her). I even came pretty close to realizing the dream of being a published novelist. But after three unpublished novels, two of which received much attention from New York agents but were sadly never picked up, I had an opportunity to hearken back to my journalism roots and write a nonfiction book, which to my great fortune and personal pleasure was published almost immediately. That book was *The Zen Teacher: Creating Focus, Simplicity, and Tranquility in the Classroom.*

I had to recognize that, despite my own personal desires, my path was changing, and I realized it would be smart to listen. Instead of fighting and resisting, I decided I'd better go where my writing was leading me. So now I'm focusing again on my earliest writing successes by re-embracing journalism and exercising that old muscle.

Yes, writing is a path, and as such, you can expect twists and turns in the road. It's not so much about desire or goals or achievement; it's more about using words to make sense of this crazy world and getting our thoughts down in a way that allows us to reflect and ponder and, with luck, understand and appreciate what is going on around us. The genre, the style, or the type of writing is, in the end, fairly beside the point.

Just share what you think.

Share what you feel.

Share what you know.

Practice documenting your life by crafting words that illuminate your experience.

That's where mindfulness comes in.

Mindfulness is the practice of experiencing the present moment without focusing on past issues and mistakes or worrying about what will happen in the future. The only moment we have, the only reality we are living in or, in truth, *can* live in, is this moment right now.

So we might as well do our writing from that place.

Writing can be an extraordinarily mindful experience. Since mindfulness concerns immersing yourself in the present moment to the point where you start to lose the sense of "self" and are completely in tune with the activity you are practicing, writing is a natural practice for doing just that. Put less abstractly, psychology professor Mihaly Csikszentmihalyi referred to what he called "flow," which is when you are in a state of such optimal experience that everything else fades away and you are totally consumed with the process of what you are doing.

When you hear of musicians or artists or athletes being so in tune with their art or music or sport that they are "in the zone," this is akin to flow and what can happen in a successful writing practice. You've probably experienced this before. A gardener friend may at first neglect to answer your call and then say, "I'm sorry; I was out in the garden, and I lost all track of time," and you realize that is exactly what you do with your hobby. Your gardener friend knows exactly what it's like to be so "in the moment" that every ounce of focus is consumed by watering the geraniums or pruning the hydrangeas.

And so do you.

And so do writers.

In the 1920s, Eugen Herrigel traveled to Japan to learn to be an archer. Not just so he could become more skilled or learn to hit a bull's-eye better, but because he wanted to learn a Zen practice where he might lose his sense of "self" and connect more with the moment before him. Fortunately, he chronicled his journey in a book called *Zen and the Art of Archery*.

As an educator, you can create an environment in the classroom where your students become so lost in the activity of writing that they look up when the bell rings, wondering where the time has gone. But to do this, you must attach what they are writing about to what engages them, to their passions, to topics and prompts that will make them want to express themselves on paper and lose all track of time and space. At this level of writing, they experience the Zen of creative expression.

But can students really achieve a flow state when drafting formal essays on *Romeo and Juliet* or research papers on the types of government in World War II Europe or timed writings for the SAT or AP tests? These assignments are necessary and important, but for writing to become a mindful practice for your students where you help them find "the Zen in their pen," it requires that they write often and at times with freedom and abandon.

While this may go against the current and common expectations education has that are associated with standards and the standardized tests that accompany them, it is perfectly in tune with what will make your students better communicators and, more importantly, feed their souls—an experience that is invaluable in life, though much, much harder to capture via a Scantron sheet or online assessment.

Like many Zen pursuits, mindful writing (and the teaching of mindful writing) begins with structure and some fundamental ideas of how to do what you do.

Guiding Principles Assignments

Spend some time thinking about writing.

1. If you DON'T write, ask yourself: Why not? Would there be any benefits to starting? What would your writing practice look like? What obstacles are keeping you from putting pen to paper or fingers to keyboard? What if you started small and built from there?

2. If you DO write, ask yourself: Why do I write? What is my end goal? Do I want to write for fun, therapy, or discipline? Or am I interested in publishing? Does my writing practice need to be adjusted in any way? Should I write more? Less? Earlier in the day? Later in the day?

Planning

CHAPTER 3

Thinking

Thinking is underrated.

As teachers and writers, we don't do it nearly enough.

Mindful writers, however, understand that taking the proper time to think about the message before committing words to paper can work in their favor. Smart writers, whether teachers or students, allow their ideas to simmer and marinate in their brains before giving them life on the page. To maximize this predominantly cerebral process, writers often find a place to be alone, to be silent and still, and give themselves a chance to think. Silence and stillness are two of the hallmarks of a mindful and Zen-inspired practice, even when it comes to writing.

Contrast this with the modern American elementary or secondary classroom. Teachers often have so much to do in their classrooms and so much curriculum to cover that they aren't able to give their young charges the time they need to just sit and percolate. The students have no opportunity to take risks and experiment. To try and fail. To stare off into space until that one crystalline idea they've been waiting for makes its grand entrance. Instead, it's more like an assembly line or factory where we feel pressured to put out the next product because the Man (principal or superintendent, male or female) is breathing down our necks. And then teachers wonder why their young charges' final products come out so half-baked and uninspired. In short, unless we prioritize it and plan for silence and stillness, it doesn't happen.

But what if we gave our students more time to think?

What if we valued thought and reflection and prioritized it as a practice?

What then?

What if we modeled thinking for our students and showed them, even when it often looks as if all we are doing is staring out into space, that there is important work—whether it's developing thoughtful details, identifying critical relationships, or making wise connections between ideas—happening in our minds while we just sit there, seemingly inert.

In these situations, the work is being done just as surely and practically as it's done by the muscle-bound man or woman swinging the sledgehammer in the quarry.

Not allowing enough time for writing students to think is rooted, like many writing challenges, in insecurity and fear.

I can hear teachers wondering, "But what do I do if my students aren't on task? What if my students *say* they're thinking, but, in reality, they are just wasting the time I give them to think?"

This will happen. But in mindful writing, there is no judgment. So they didn't spend their time thinking during this particular class period. So what? Their grade will probably reflect that, and they will most likely make a different choice next time.

But what about that noble student who *is* thinking?

The good news is that you've provided that human being with an opportunity to do better work than he or she has ever done on a writing assignment, and he or she will be grateful to you, and the final product will reflect that thoughtful time. I can almost guarantee that the piece will be better than if the student wasn't allowed a proper amount of time for reflection. Like fine wine or tasty cheese, our thoughts, ideas, and details often benefit from careful aging . . . and a little nurturing. And this aging and nurturing should happen *before* we commit a single letter to the blinking cursor.

CHAPTER 4

Woolgathering

In the old days, when someone wanted to knit a sweater, the first thing they had to do was gather the wool. Naturally enough, this process was known as "woolgathering."

I'm sure you would agree that you can't knit a sweater until you gather the wool. But the thing is, gathering wool doesn't look like knitting. It probably doesn't look like much of anything at all other than, possibly, simply annoying the local sheep.

And yet the eventual knitting of the sweater can't be done without it.

The same is true with "woolgathering" in writing.

There are many tasks, activities, and approaches that must happen before you start typing a single word, and writers call that "woolgathering."

When I got serious about writing this book, for example, I sat down at my laptop, cranked out two hundred words, then spent the rest of the writing session researching, taking notes, and outlining the rest of the book.

Guess what?

That's still writing.

I didn't type another word that would end up in the final manuscript, but the notes I took, the quotes I researched, and the outline I made structuring the rest of the book were crucial steps in making the whole project happen.

Let's take this to a whole other level: somewhere between saying "I'm going to write a book" and putting your fingertips on the keyboard a lot of thinking needs to be done.

Still writing.

Imagine walking into Stephen King's writing studio. You may see him sitting there, feet up on the desk, twirling a Ticonderoga pencil in his hand, staring at the ceiling. And if you said, "Hey, Steve! Whatchoo doin'?"

I guarantee you he would say, "I'm writing."

It may not look like writing. But I also guarantee that as he twirls that top-of-the-line pencil he is imagining a scene with a parrot that comes back to life, a haunted disco, a possessed toaster, or whatever other monstrosities he's going to bring to life next.

So don't feel bad if you ever find yourself just sitting there and it looks like you're not doing anything.

If you're thinking about how the project needs to go, you're writing. As a bonus, sitting and thinking, reflecting, and considering is also an incredibly mindful experience—whether or not you ever end up with a written product at the end of it. And if it moves you toward a completed piece of writing you (or your students) are proud of? So much the better.

Here are some things that don't look like writing, but certainly are:

- Thinking
- Walking

- Sitting in a chair staring into space
- Taking notes
- Revising
- Researching
- Thinking in the shower
- Thinking of your writing project before you fall asleep at night
- And millions of other activities that have nothing to do with actually typing words into your Word, Google, or Scrivener doc

In some cases, talking about writing can also be writing—especially if you're bouncing stuff off another writer, and he or she is helping you understand how to work out a plot point or a sticky bit of rhetoric.

The danger, however, is that sometimes it's easy to use these activities as procrastination, as reasons *not* to write or to avoid putting words on the page. In other words, it gets easy to take notes on stuff you don't need and research online until you find yourself on YouTube looking at cat videos, old George Carlin and Richard Pryor concerts, or episodes of *Barney Miller* (I feel so called out!), when you should be creating words and sentences.

It takes practice, but one key skill as a writer is to recognize when you're doing this. And then to shake yourself out of it and start typing.

I put this chapter in the planning section of this book because we technically haven't written anything yet, but I could also put a chapter about thinking and researching in the section on drafting.

Why?

Because I believe that woolgathering has more to do with the actual writing than it does with planning, which is the step before. Woolgathering most often happens after planning and before the actual writing. But the main reason I'm putting it in this section is that you can be 125 pages into a three-hundred-page manuscript and still need to pause (notice I said *pause* and not *stop*) and take time to be mindful and think deeply about what you're trying to say and do. As it turns out, though, woolgathering can happen at any point—or even at *many* points—in the process.

During the woolgathering process, you might ask yourself questions such as:

Does this section work?

Does the writing flow?

Did I miss anything?

Is there a logical progression of ideas?

In fact, woolgathering just might be one of the most mindful parts of writing—that moment when you're just sitting there, in the present, trying to figure out what this whole project is going to look like.

What it is you're *actually* trying to say.

What's it all about.

But woolgathering can't, and shouldn't, take forever.

Get your wool, for sure.

Prepare it.

Treat it.

Then sit down at the typer, as Charles Bukowski used to call it, get your fingers poised, and start knitting.

CHAPTER 5

Nonjudgment

One of the most powerful and life-changing philosophies in the Zen tradition is the concept of "nonjudgment." With Zen, the moment is as it is, and the moment is as the universe intended it to be. Though sometimes challenging, our job is to accept our day-to-day moments and let them be what they are without the white noise of making a judgment or creating an attachment. Learning to accept what life throws at us without judgment can be a tall order, but it ultimately helps us decrease stress and can create more peace in our lives.

Adopting a nonjudgmental approach is also critical in writing, especially when it comes to prewriting or planning. As you start to structure your piece, do not be afraid to include any idea that arises—no matter how seemingly silly, off topic, or irrelevant. The prewriting/planning step is the time to be all-inclusive and not judgmental, critical, or dismissive.

By the time you finish writing, the same idea you might have nixed during the prewriting/planning stages as wrong or too "out there" might prove to be one of the key ideas or passages in the entire piece that gives it its depth and meaning.

Ideas come from the subconscious. There is no telling what subliminal connections we are making as we plan and how those ideas might connect later. We owe it to ourselves, then, not to edit our subliminal hamsters running on those subconscious wheels. What they come up with might sound crazy at first glance, but as we make progress through our writing project, we might thank the hamsters as we see how the dots begin to connect.

As I watch my students plan their essays, I often hear them say, "Nah, that's stupid. That'll never work" and then scribble the idea out or erase it completely.

What they don't realize is that the idea they just erased might possibly be their unconscious drawing connections they don't see at first. Connections that can later make the paper more thoughtful, more in-depth. And they'll never know that if the idea is shot down before they even give it a chance to blossom.

It's true that in most writing projects, you will end up with scads of ideas that never make it past the drawing board. The magic of writing often comes down to the skill and grace and art of selection—which details will we include, which will we exclude? But the planning stage is not the time to be making those decisions. That comes later in the process.

What would happen, I wonder, if we practiced letting every idea in—if only at the beginning of our process? The worst-case scenario is that we have more ideas to work with. More directions to choose from when we finally put pen to paper or fingers to keyboard.

The best-case scenario is that we get practice exercising the muscle that gives us ideas—and make no mistake, it *is* a muscle that grows stronger with use and when it is exercised. Eventually, more ideas will occur to us more naturally, and more and more of them will need to be discarded.

Let the ideas come and put them down.

Does the nonjudgmental approach have its limits?

Of course it does.

If you're writing a piece about the challenges of parenthood, and suddenly your mind flashes on muscle cars or Pokémon, there probably isn't much of a reason to jot those ideas down. But if your mind suddenly flashes to your recent visit to the zoo, you might want to consider that. Maybe you saw an interaction between a mama monkey and her little monkey spawn that is worthy of a little more research and might add another layer to your exploration of parental challenges. If you follow that thread a little longer (and later in the process), you just might find that your gut was trying to tell you something. Or it might be a dead end that wastes your time and energy.

But that's how most research goes.

So put it down. Include it.

If you never use it in the final piece, you can always cross it out, ignore it, or set it on fire later.

But in the beginning of the process, it pays to be open to the ideas that come rushing up from your subliminal thoughts, your subconscious, and your intuition—because that's the part of you that processes things in your sleep and in your dreams. And if you think of how singularly fantastic *those* ideas can be, you know that including all ideas just might result in a final writing product that is a smooth blend of every thoughtful impulse you have and will result in the creation of your own specific, unique voice.

CHAPTER 6

The Ugly Prewrite

In my three decades as an educator, I have spent over ten years as a private tutor. Test prep, mostly. For years, I helped students prepare for the SAT and ACT and other standardized tests. That's where I realized the importance of the Ugly Prewrite.

When I started tutoring the SAT so many years ago, there was an essay writing section. Students had to write a multi-paragraph essay in twenty-five minutes, which is crazy fast. So I spent a substantial amount of time talking about planning and prewriting, a step that—let's face it—even on the SAT, most students skipped. And yet planning was critical, maybe even more so than on an untimed essay.

Prewriting and planning takes many forms: bubble clusters/mind mapping, outlines, columns, brainstorm lists, etc. The method doesn't matter, as long as you plan.

What I learned is that the standardized test prep kids were a little different from most students. They were motivated, driven, and usually quite determined to do their best on these tests. They had been conditioned, however erroneously, to believe that their futures depended on the outcomes of their test scores. This wasn't true, but it was how they were conditioned.

Being the driven, hardworking students they were, whenever I put them on the clock and they started to plan, they would create elaborate prewriting. They used whole sheets of notebook paper, busted out rulers to draw perfectly complementary lines, and wrote lengthy descriptions. My job was to take them from creating perfectly sculpted, 8–10 minute prewrites down to a slapdash three-minute prewrite where they just got some rough ideas down and had an overall vision, so that they could start writing.

Take for example, Rosa Parks. If they decided they were going to write about Rosa Parks, they would write out her full name and then compose at least one sentence, more often several, talking about who she was and her contribution to the civil rights movement.

"You don't have that kind of time," I would tell them.

"Then what should I write?" they'd say, genuinely bewildered.

"All you need to write is *RP*," I'd say. "That's it."

Their eyes would get as big as hubcaps.

"Listen," I'd say. "You know what *RP* means. All the other information you need is already in your head. Just write down the bare minimum to jog your thoughts, and trust your mind, your experience, and your writing skill to provide the rest when it's time to write. Save the detail and description for the actual composition."

Here's the thing: the prewrite is only for you.

No one else is going to see it.

So plan. But plan smart.

If you have more time, take it.

But you may not need it.

Your "on paper" plan doesn't have to be pretty.

In fact, not only *can* it be quite ugly, it probably *should* be.

Neither Philip Roth nor Barbara Kingsolver ever won a Pulitzer or Nobel Prize based on the strength of his or her prewrite.

I do ugly prewriting for everything I write. For this book, it wasn't clean, it wasn't pretty.

It was quick and dirty.

But it got the job done.

And then when I sat down to write, all I had to do, much like my SAT kids, was to connect the detail and description to my ideas and run with it.

CHAPTER 7

Prewriting

Let's face it: Abraham Lincoln was a badass. He knew how critical preparation was for any important project. Lincoln, who was usually considered a wise man and a pretty chill dude, once said, "Give me six hours to cut down a tree and I will spend the first four sharpening the ax." In other words, you must make sure that each of your tools is in proper working order and that you have a general game plan so that you know where you're going. This is the essence of the prewrite, and for me, one of the hardest parts of teaching writing has always been getting my students to understand its importance.

If we think of writing as a process with several steps involved, and not just the single step of *writing*, then starting with a plan is crucial. My students, though, tend to want to forge ahead and start putting their thoughts down on paper with very little idea of where they're going or where they might end up. I don't blame them, because I was the same way as a teen. While I admire the spontaneity, the approach is misguided. Before jumping into any important activity, it's usually best to do a little planning. Think about pruning bonsai trees. Long before you start snipping branches, you probably want to have at least some idea of what shape you're going for. It's all about envisioning the final product.

Prewriting is the place to create a sort of on-ramp to the writing process, where writers can be a bit messier, more curious, and more exploratory. It's one place to take chances before your words are set in stone and when you can still change your approach without too many sunk costs of time or energy. I've written pages and pages before that I've had to delete (or, if they were printed, simply toss) because my up-front planning was not thorough enough. It's not fun. In addition to scribbling notes and mapping an overall path, there may be reading, research, or conversations with trusted colleagues or peers involved. This is the incubation stage, and generally speaking, all of it precedes any "actual" writing.

As the prefix *pre-* suggests, prewriting happens *before* you write. Prewriting can take many forms, and it may accomplish many purposes. The key is to know why you're prewriting or planning, to find a way that works for you. You may need to design the overall structure for your piece, outline your major ideas, lay out your supporting evidence, or develop a thesis. Why you prewrite or plan is not as important as actually doing it. This is the sharpening of the ax of which Lincoln spoke. And if you ask the people who heard him in Gettysburg, the dude seemed to know as much about writing as he did about forestry.

Here Are Four Basic Forms of Prewriting:

Bubble clusters/Mind-mapping. While I tend to think in more of a linear/sequential manner (I'm totally a list man), this method works best for those who think spatially. In it, you put your main idea or major thesis in a central bubble and branch out from there, filling the rest of the bubbles with subordinate ideas (think body paragraphs or topic sentences) and supporting evidence. This can give you a graphic representation of how your piece will be structured before you start.

It might look something like this:

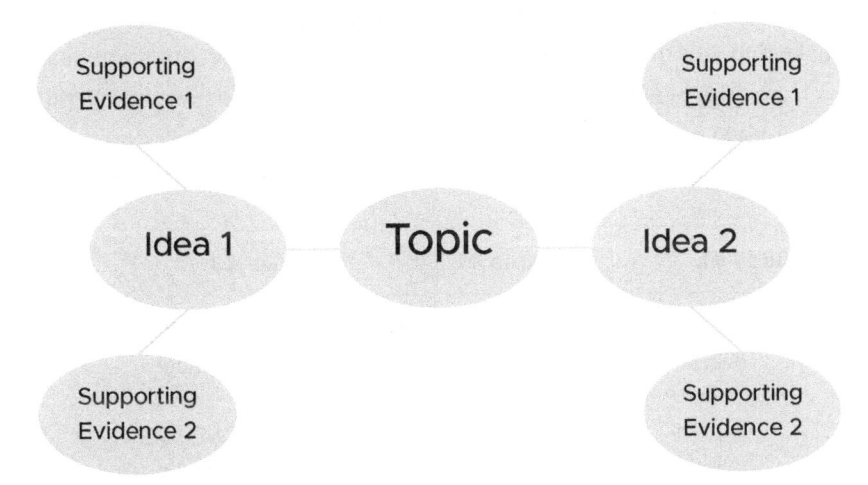

```
Supporting                                    Supporting
Evidence 1                                    Evidence 1


    Idea 1           Topic            Idea 2


Supporting                                    Supporting
Evidence 2                                    Evidence 2
```

Outline. If you're interested in a more traditional, old-school approach, you can create a basic outline for what you plan to write. As you may remember from learning the five-paragraph essay from your English teacher in middle school or high school, an outline looks something like this:

Main Idea:

I. Subordinate idea
    a. Supporting evidence
    b. Supporting evidence

II. Subordinate idea
    a. Supporting evidence
    b. Supporting evidence

III. Subordinate idea
    a. Supporting evidence
    b. Supporting evidence

Columns. For my money, one of the easiest and clearest ways to plan a piece of writing is to use columns to separate your sections or ideas. In a prewrite using columns, you simply split up your paragraphs, sections, or ideas into distinct columns and then work your subordinate ideas or supporting evidence into each of the separate columns and, in this way, design the overall structure of your piece. The number of columns you make depends on the number of ideas, paragraphs, or sections you plan to have. The benefit is that it's simple and easy to envision the overall structure at a glance.

A column-based prewriting may look something like this:

Idea #1	Idea #2	Idea #3
a. Supporting evidence	a. Supporting evidence	a. Supporting evidence
b. Supporting evidence	b. Supporting evidence	b. Supporting evidence

Listing/Brainstorming. One last, exceptionally organic method of prewriting is brainstorming or listing. In this method, you simply list each and every idea that occurs to you about your topic. List each idea without criticism or editing. *Everything* is fair game. To keep track of your ideas, use bullets, dashes, asterisks, numbers, or whatever else floats your boat. You may then wish, after making the list, to group your ideas into various categories or patterns.

A brainstorm/list prewrite on this book might look like this:

- Prewriting
- Nonjudgment
- Passion
- Precision
- Clarity
- Zen practice
- Daydreaming

Prewriting is a critical step for every single project I write. Whenever I begin a new novel, for example, I write what in the screenwriting world is called a "treatment"—a linear narrative that tells the story I want to tell in the novel, just not in individual scenes yet. It's basically a summary of plot. Whenever I write a nonfiction book, however, I buy a binder and fill it with loose-leaf notebook paper. On each piece of paper, I write a title or idea for a potential chapter. As ideas for each chapter occur to me, I write notes on the page for the pertinent chapter. I also include any inspirational quotes, research, or authority figures I run across that I think might be useful for each chapter.

For this book, I used the brainstorm/list method. I came up with over fifty chapter ideas, and after splitting the ideas into the steps in the writing process (designing the overall structure, another form of prewriting), I typed out a brainstorm list of the order of the chapters. *All of this before writing a single word of the book.* I even outlined this particular chapter on the page as I was typing to get a sense of where this chapter was going to go. Prewriting about prewriting. How meta! By doing this, I knew if I hit the various beats of the chapter I envisioned, then I would be heading in the right direction.

Each year I try to impress upon my students the importance of planning before writing, but they seem to view it as a waste of time and just want to jump directly into expressing their ideas. When they do some planning, however, their improved grades, greater satisfaction, and sharpened skills often reflect their prewriting efforts. And when they don't do it, that is often reflected in the final product as well.

Danny's Writing Diary:

It Started with Emma

My writing career started with Emma.

In 1973, I fell hard for Emma C., one of my classmates in Mrs. Smith's fourth-grade class. Emma had beautiful, chestnut-colored hair and wore ribbons in it every day. She was also one of the snappiest dressers in our class. She was bright, funny, and, most importantly, extremely kind. We would hang out on the playground at recess and talk. She was an amazing listener and tolerated my nine-year-old-boy shenanigans. She seemed perfect to me, a vision, so much so that at one point I mustered up the courage to ask her to be my girlfriend. To my nine-year-old astonishment, she agreed.

There was only one catch.

"You have to ask my dad," she said.

Of course I'd heard of this kind of thing from television, but what did it mean?

What was I expected to do? To say?

I wanted to do the right thing by Emma, so I was about to find out.

One afternoon I found myself sitting in Emma's living room, across from her father and mother, who were on the sofa. Her father was in the navy, and, oddly enough, I don't recall feeling particularly nervous or scared. Probably because I didn't have the slightest idea that I should be. So after some greetings and small talk , when it was clear that it was my turn to make my request, I told Emma's father that I would like for his daughter to be my girlfriend.

"What do you think that would entail?" he asked, leaning forward.

I didn't know there was going to be a quiz. My nine-year-old brain spun.

I was suddenly painfully aware that I had no idea what boyfriends and girlfriends did. I had no idea what they were supposed to do or what was supposed to happen.

"Uh, I'd like to hang out with her at school, I guess, visit her here sometimes, give her gifts, I guess." I shrugged. "Like that." I paused. "She said I had to ask you."

So my first official duty as Emma's boyfriend was to throw her directly under the bus.

Mr. C. looked at Mrs. C., and then he looked back at me.

It was his turn to shrug.

"Fine with me," he said.

And that's how Emma C. became my girlfriend.

It's also how I became a writer.

I remember grabbing one of the giant blue elementary school pencils and a sheet of that elementary school paper with the giant lines on it—you know, that beige paper with the giant lines where you could see the wood chips embedded in it—and decided I was going to write Emma a poem.

I've written approximately four million poems since then, but when I wrote the title at the top of the paper, "The Special One," it was the beginning.

The first poem I ever wrote for someone—and very possibly the first poem I ever wrote—was for Emma.

That was forty-eight years ago.

I haven't stopped since.

Planning Assignments

1. Spend some time simply thinking about your project. Just thinking. What kind of piece is it? What genre? First or third person? What is it really about? What structure will it take? Will the sections and chapters be connected thematically? Chronologically? Via stream-of-consciousness? Will it be formal? Informal? Serious? Humorous? Do all of this while sitting at your desk with your feet up, wandering around your two-bedroom apartment, washing your car, or taking a long walk around the neighborhood.

2. Do an Ugly Prewrite. Make it as quick and dirty as possible. There may or may not be a discernible structure. Maybe it's another outline. Maybe it's just a list. Take no more than five minutes. Then do another one. Then another one. You've now lost only fifteen minutes of your life. Look at your Ugly Prewrites. Which prewrite do you like best? Which one best represents your project?

3. Using one of the prewriting methods listed (bubble cluster, outline, columns, or brainstorm list), do a prewriting for an upcoming writing project you've been thinking about. If it's a story, poem, or article, prewriting should take no longer than ten minutes. Remember: there is no judgment involved, no right or wrong. At this point, any ideas are good ideas, and all thoughts are valid. In a brainstorm list, everything is a go.

Drafting

CHAPTER 8

Beginner's Mind

It should no longer be news, dear reader, that a skillful piece of writing takes multiple drafts. But that doesn't mean the drafting is easy. Sometimes it can be downright intimidating. Why? Because no matter how many times you end up in front of a clean sheet of paper or a blank screen, you must accept that each writing project is going to be a little different. No two pieces are the same. Each assignment or writing task has its own structure, rhythm, and set of expectations. This is normal; it is the way of things. So the only approach we can take is to recognize this fact, breathe, start writing, and stay calm.

Recently I saw a meme that said, "Be brave enough to suck at something new." But the irony is that this—trying something new and getting comfortable with the discomfort of that newness—is the thing we suck at.

In our culture, shooting for perfection is the norm. We try to make things perfect right out of the gate. But where writing (and mindfulness, for that matter) is concerned, this is the wrong approach.

In Zen, "beginner's mind" refers to the practice of approaching a situation with an open mind, a vulnerable heart, and a willingness to learn. It means that, as an artist, you come to the table with the perspective of a student—open, receptive, willing to be molded—and you begin your task with as few preconceived notions as possible.

There's nothing wrong with wanting to do your best and to produce good work, but often, in the beginning of a writing project, we're merely trying to get our bearings. And that's fine. It's often only later in the piece that we are able to figure out what we are trying to say. Before we know our course, it's frequently necessary to gather wool, to ramble, to clear our throats, to fiddle around, to see where things can go. And while we should not pursue perfection, it's helpful if we know our general direction, even if, like jazz musicians, we take improvisational and indirect routes to get there.

Planning helps, but approaching each piece of writing with an open and vulnerable perspective keeps our writing fresh and new.

It's been said that ideas are easy to come by, but ideas are nothing without execution. And that's why it's so challenging for our students (and often ourselves) to move beyond the thinking and planning stage and start typing. Somehow, seeing the letters showing up on the page, one after another, makes our ideas real and gives our thoughts gravity, and that can be terrifying.

Writing, therefore, is an incredible act of bravery.

And bravery takes practice.

Especially when you feel like you're starting from scratch every single time.

In the average English class, students are often expected to read a novel or a nonfiction article and then write a literature-based essay. Read something, write something. Lather. Rinse. Repeat. By following this pattern, it's easy for student writers to get in a rut, especially when, as teachers, we insist there is only one way to structure that piece (think:

five-paragraph essay). Sometimes, just to mix it up, a more enlightened teacher may ask them to write a personal piece so they can open up a bit and say something about themselves. And once or twice a year, the student may have to take a stand in an argumentative piece or write about something controversial. And usually no more than a handful of times in an entire middle school or high school career, a student may be asked to do a research-style paper. At least that's been my experience. Your mileage may vary.

In each of these situations, it can be easy for students to see a writing opportunity as just another writing requirement, another day in the salt mines of the Composition Factory.

But even if your student is merely writing yet another five-paragraph essay—and even if it is just another in an endless string of five-paragraph essays in his or her high school career—each one will be different and require a different approach. There will be a different origin—*Romeo and Juliet* versus *The Great Gatsby*, for example, or argumentative versus narrative, perhaps. Beginner's mind tells us that the idea is *not* to say, "I've done this before," or "Here we go again." The trick is to be open to the needs, rhythm, and structure of *this* particular piece of writing, to ask ourselves "How should *this* one go?" and "What does *this* piece of writing need?"

Author and creativity expert Austin Kleon wrote a blog post where he quotes author and essayist Mike Monteiro saying, "The secret to being good at anything is to approach it like a curious idiot, rather than a know-it-all genius."

I'm not sure I've heard a better definition of beginner's mind. And though I try to adopt Monteiro's approach as frequently as possible, some have suggested that the former might come to me a little more naturally than the latter.

Each writing assignment, then, is an opportunity to get our students to explore, to take a stand, to express an idea, to learn something about themselves, or to share their hearts and minds.

By allowing ourselves to approach each new assignment as a fresh opportunity to share and learn, we can get excited about the chance to write and communicate and share our wisdom and vulnerability with the world.

Students may start out fearful of the process, but when we show them that writing can be a liberating act of awe and wonder, many of them will eventually realize that there is, in fact, a net to catch them, and that we will not let them fall. We start this education by communicating to them the knowledge that *no* writer knows what they are doing when they begin a new piece. Not even Shakespeare. Not even Anne Lamott. Not even David Sedaris.

Maybe even *especially* David Sedaris.

I remember when my daughter first started driving, I tried to explain to her the contradiction of getting behind the wheel. But it wasn't easy.

"Sure," I said, "it's possible to drive all the way to your destination and think back and have no idea, no memory of what just happened. That's one of the quirks of driving. But what's also true—and much scarier—is that no matter how many times you've driven to your school or the church or the 7-Eleven down the street, each time you turn the key in the ignition, it is a new situation and *anything* can happen."

This is also true with writing.

It's super easy to sit down at the keyboard every morning and say, "I've done this before. Here we go again."

Even your students will do this.

They'll say, "I wrote an essay on the Civil War. Now I have to write one on mitosis. It's all writing. What's the difference?"

Even if you've written jillions of poems, thousands of stories, and drawerfuls of unpublished novels, each new writing project has its own style, structure, and set of problems. In true yin-yang fashion, it also has its own joys, insights, and revelations. We need to be humble enough to get out of the way of the words and let each piece of writing be what it wants to be.

Be forewarned: this is not fun.

But if you want to succeed at writing, you must detach from your ego long enough to see that writing something is a unique experience each and every time.

When you sit down at the desk, each time you are, in essence, doing so for the first time. You are facing a new page and have new ideas and need to choose the best and most effective way to express those ideas.

What would it look like if you simply dropped your expectations or preconceived ideas of what a piece of writing should look like, should do, should be?

Isn't that a freeing notion?

Leo Babauta, founder of the mindfulness website *Zen Habits*, explains it this way: with beginner's mind, he says, "You aren't clouded by prejudgments, preconceptions, fantasies about what it should be or assumptions about how you already know it will be. When you don't have these, *you can't be disappointed or frustrated* by the experience, because there's no fantasy or preconception to compare it to."

With beginner's mind, it is also expected that you will not be attaching your worth to what you're doing. In other words, you are not the end product. You are merely the conduit to unleash those ideas into a world waiting for your wisdom and insight. Your personal worth has nothing to do with the product you produce; your craft is more about the commitment to an ongoing practice of writing.

Approaching each new writing project with an open mind is a critical step in seeing it go where you want it to go, in accomplishing what you wish to accomplish. By doing so, you create space for the universe to send you the right words and ideas to communicate exactly what you hope to communicate, although I confess that sometimes it does not feel that way.

When you sit down at the keyboard, see the blinking cursor (or fountain pen or pencil) with fresh eyes, try your hardest to look at the page as if it's the first time you've ever written anything on a blank sheet of paper because, in many ways, it is.

CHAPTER 9

Five Hundred Words

I have been in our English department for over thirty years, and for as long as I can remember, we have given our students a reasonable goal: essay body paragraphs should be a minimum of 150 words. It's a small, manageable goal they can reach. Some students still struggle with this, of course. But with enough time and practice, most of them eventually meet the quota. Being instructed in the expectations of the department as a young teacher, I almost immediately understood intuitively the wisdom in creating a word count requirement instead of, say, a sentence requirement (though we experimented with that as well). Having a word count requirement not only gave students something to shoot for, but it could take many forms and go in many directions. It gave them freedom to explore their thoughts. But sometimes even the most reasonable goals can be challenging.

During the early stages of drafting, the same holds true: even the most practical objectives are hard to meet. That's when it becomes necessary to "chunk it down" and reduce the project to its manageable parts. I have written a file cabinet full of book manuscripts, and yet the idea of writing an entire book always, without fail, totally overwhelms me—*despite the fact* that I've written so many. So I always do a little number on myself psychologically. "I don't need to write an entire book," I tell myself. "I just need to write this essay." And then, if that gets overwhelming, I say, "All I need to do is write this one page." And if even that kicks up my anxiety, I say, "All I have to do is write this one paragraph." And when I'm not entirely sure what I want to say, I tell myself, "All I have to do is write a single sentence—just write the next sentence that makes sense." As Ernest Hemingway famously said, "All you have to do is write one true sentence. Write the truest sentence that you know."

And when I write that single true sentence, it's always easier to write more of them. One sentence invariably leads to another. Those sentences then lead to a page. Then, once I write enough pages, I have an essay or a story. And if I write thirty or forty stories or essays over time—voilà! I have a book!

It's magic.

Except it's really not.

It's discipline.

It's habit and commitment. Plus time.

It's putting your butt in the chair (more on that later) and typing.

It's having a reasonable goal for output.

I didn't have a lot of extra time when I set out to write this book. After some false starts, my plan was to arrive in my classroom thirty minutes early a few times a week and write what I could. The miracle is that small effort over time adds up, and before long, the pages started piling up on my desk.

It never, ever starts with a complete manuscript, though. On those mornings when the alarm on my phone goes off thirty minutes early, I have a very simple goal: five hundred words. I know I'm not going to write an entire book in thirty minutes. But over time, a creative synergy occurs, and those five hundred words, when multiplied over days and weeks, become larger than the sum of their parts and ultimately transform into a body of work.

Sitting down and cranking out a few words in each session won't end with your finished novel or story, and for your students, it won't end with their completed essays. But the beautiful part is that, even though I haven't finished an entire book, I have experienced one of the most mindful moments I'll have during my entire day.

And it starts with five hundred words.

Or two hundred.

Or one hundred.

Or fifty.

The magic is that when we break large, hairy, scary goals down into manageable chunks, anything is possible.

When it goes well, and the neurons are firing, and the ideas (not to mention the words) are coming, I might do eight hundred words or a thousand words or sometimes, on a good day, even fifteen hundred words. But sometimes I only get ninety-nine words. And if those ninety-nine words are pretty decent, I figure I'll take it, and I walk away from the keyboard satisfied because overall I will keep an average of five hundred words per writing session, and that's all I'm asking for.

Five hundred words may not sound like much, but if you keep doing it, you'll make progress.

Eventually, something will happen.

And even if you can't write five hundred words, you can do research or conduct an interview or take some notes or brainstorm a list or outline a chapter.

No matter how scared or intimidated you are, there is always something you can do to move the project forward.

Today's haul: 683 words.

Now, coffee.

Danny's Writing Diary:

Super

What it really boiled down to is that I hadn't done my schoolwork.

It was 1974, and even though I liked my fifth-grade teacher, I had apparently been neglecting my regular assignments for some time.

In a gesture that conflicted wildly with my own current teaching policy, my teacher, Mrs. Theroux, gave me an extra credit option.

There was no judgment. No criticism. No stern lecture.

She simply said that if I wanted to make up the points, I had to write something.

I asked her what I should write, and she said it was up to me.

I took that opportunity to work on an idea that had been percolating in my head for some time. It was the story of a millionaire playboy named Barney Brown, whose crime-fighting alter ego was named Super.

Not Superman.

Not Super This or Super That.

Just Super.

I grabbed a pencil and a sheet of that brown-lined paper that I had written the poem to Emma on the year before, and I began to write.

The premise of the story was that a top-secret formula had been stolen from ACME Labs, and Police Chief Green called Super for help. (Barney Brown. Chief Green. Clearly, I was in my "color" phase as an author.) By the end of the story, the culprit turned himself in. In the story, he turned himself in because he was overwhelmed by the formula, the only purpose of which, as it turned out, was to make you on-the-floor drunk. The real reason the thief turned himself in, however, was because I was only ten years old, and I had zero idea how to plot a mystery.

I got lost in the story, however, and when I was done, I counted twenty-three hand-written pages.

That had to be some kind of record for fiction writing at the fifth-grade level. I'm willing to bet that not even Kurt Vonnegut or Virginia Woolf had ever written twenty-three pages in fifth grade.

And Virginia Woolf even had a room of her own.

I had to share one with my brother.

After stapling the pages of the story together, I turned it into Mrs. Theroux and promptly forgot about it, much more interested in the giant papier-mâché giraffe we were constructing in the back of the classroom.

After a while, Mrs. Theroux returned my manuscript.

The only marks on the entire thing were a giant A+ in a circle and a note in her handwriting at the bottom of the page.

The note said:

Very good story, Dan. You have a very imaginative and witty mind. I have a feeling you are going to go a long way with your writing abilities. Keep improving and practicing.

Come to me, and I'll show you how to write quotes correctly. Excellent job.

The extra credit didn't matter.

Even the neglected assignments didn't matter.

It was Mrs. Theroux's note that mattered. In fact, it changed my life. It molded and shaped me in a way that almost nothing else in my education has, and I've been writing ever since.

I still have that story, of course. That's how I can quote Mrs. Theroux's note verbatim. That was forty-seven years ago, and that *collection of yellowing and crumbling pages is a treasured artifact in the footlocker that houses all my writing.*

Like me, it's older, a little beat up, and rougher around the edges, but I still read Mrs. Theroux's praise for my writing abilities sometimes, and it never fails to puff me up with pride and confidence about what I can do with words.

That's the impact that one note by one teacher on one assignment can make in a person's life.

What you're doing with your students—and what you say to them—matters.

Never forget that.

CHAPTER 10

Wind Sprints

In eighth grade I was the fastest boy in middle school. When we ran the track in gym class, I came in first.

Every. Single. Time.

I thought I was a natural.

In the spring of 1978, my first year of high school, I joined the track team as a sprinter. As a now small fish in a much, much bigger pond (namely, the entire high school district), I came in last. Every. Single. Time. Except for that one glorious time I came in second to last. I probably should have mentioned earlier how teeny tiny my middle school was.

My experience on the freshman track team, over forty years ago, was the last time I ever attempted anything involving a starter gun, Adidas shoes, and those humiliating nylon shorts. But as part of our training, the coach required us to do something called "wind sprints." And, as I've learned, not only does this exercise build stamina and endurance for runners, it can also help students to be present with their writing.

In essence, a wind sprint is a short, intense burst of running that builds your strength, focus, and stamina. To the best of my recollection—and a brief Google search—wind sprints consist of brief periods of running as fast as you can, alternating with walking and/or jogging.

As torturous as I found wind sprints during my track-and-field training, I highly recommend them for young writers. In writing, a wind sprint refers to writing in short, intense, and often timed bursts. Set a timer for ten minutes, throw your students a topic or prompt, and say, "Go." It's not about quality, tone, sentence variety, or grammar. Often it's about length. I tell my students, for example, to shoot for about 150 words in a 12–15-minute period. Often it's about expression ("What are the ten most important qualities in a significant other?"). Sometimes it's about clarifying one's thinking ("Now that we've read this article, what do you think about _____?"). A writing wind sprint can be done to generate raw material for a work-in-progress or simply as an exercise to build the writing muscle.

Some teachers may call these journal entries, free writes, or quick writes. We probably all use them. But do we use them enough? Do we use them intentionally, as my track coach did, to build strength, focus, and endurance?

Possibly.

But not definitely.

Wind sprints can be less intimidating for the reluctant writer or the writer who feels he or she is experiencing writer's block, which is, of course, an illusion (see chapter 17). In her seminal book on writing, *Bird by Bird*, author Anne Lamott has a chapter called "Short Assignments," in which she talks about feeling some slight hesitancy during her writing sessions and then decides that "all I am going to do right now . . . is write that one paragraph that sets the story in my hometown, in the late fifties, when the trains were still running."

There are several amazing things about that quote. First of all, notice Lamott's incredibly specific details ("hometown," "late fifties," "trains"). She is already painting a picture for the reader that we can be certain she will flesh out as the piece takes shape. Second, she is giving herself permission not to write the entire book. That would be overwhelming. Instead, she stays in the moment. She engages in some positive self-talk and tells herself that all she needs to do is just write a little bit. In fact, I might be just a little bit in love with the phrase "all I am going to do right now." It implies a setting of boundaries and knowledge of our own limitations—what we can and cannot handle at any given time, and, as such, it is probably a good sentence starter to keep in mind for life in general: "I don't have to do all the things. All I'm going to do right now is fold the laundry." "All I am going to do right now is clean up the living room." "All I am going to right now is sit in the corner and weep." Okay, maybe that last one's just me, but you see where I'm going with this.

In terms of the writing, Lamott is talking about the importance of just getting started. That's how books get written. One chapter, one page, one sentence, one word at a time.

Want to have a more mindful writing experience?

Stop thinking about the entire piece every time you sit down to write.

Try This

One of my favorite writing activities to increase students' endurance as well as just give them some plain, old-fashioned writing practice is a writing exercise very similar to wind sprints.

Before I get to class, I write down four random and open-ended topics on three-by-five index cards. Then, when they're ready to write, I set a timer for ten minutes, pull an index card, and have students write on that topic until the timer goes off. In a typical one-hour session, we might write for three of four sessions, and then I give them the rest of the session to go back and write more on any of the topics that seemed to be going particularly well, or we may just chat about the students' writing experience.

As long as they were getting words on the page, they really couldn't do it wrong. The goal was to get them thinking and writing in short bursts.

It helps to pick topics that everyone has something to say about.

Some of the writing topics I have given them in the past have included:

- beginning and endings
- holidays
- vacations
- pets
- dreams (both goals and the kind you have when you're sleeping)
- describe your mother
- home
- childhood memories
- a place you love or hate
- the four seasons
- food
- music.

I don't mind saying that slipping in "Describe Your Mother" has been the impetus for some fascinating wind sprints (and may have resulted in my students booking a few extra sessions with their therapists), but it's such a juicy, complex topic with such potential for depth, complexity, and emotion, I can't resist.

Author E. L. Doctorow once said, "Writing is like driving at night in the fog. You can only see as far as your headlights, but you can make the whole trip that way."

And he's right: you don't need to see the entire journey.

All you have to do is move the needle forward.

Get some words on the page. Any way you can.

And if it's messy, so what?

So was crossing the finish line during those 100-yard dashes.

CHAPTER 11

Journaling as Meditation

Are you interested in the benefits of meditation but find the idea of sitting on a cushion, pillow, or yoga mat just to breathe kind of boring? Consider journaling.

Journaling can take many forms, but especially if you like writing, it can offer the same benefits as a more traditional meditation practice, and at the end of it you've actually produced a piece of writing or, at the very least, some raw material that may eventually find its way into an essay, story, poem, article, or novel. In the classroom, journaling can be especially effective as a "sponge" or "bell ringer" activity at the beginning or end of class periods.

There are a million ways to journal, and it's up to you to find the one that works for you.

But if you're thinking about creating a journaling practice, here are some suggestions to get you started:

- **Set a timer.** Much like meditation, journaling can happen during a set time, and it doesn't have to take long. Start with 5–10 minutes and see how it goes.
- **Try some "morning pages."** Write three pages, longhand, in the morning when your mind is fresh and you can let the words flow stream-of-consciousness style. There is no right or wrong way to do morning pages, according to Julia Cameron, the creator of this approach, who talks about the technique in her book *The Artist's Way*. They are not "high art," she admits, but instead, they "provoke, clarify, confront, prioritize and synchronize the day at hand." Find a journal, grab a pen, and just let loose.
- **Write about your obsessions.** What's been on your mind lately? Get it out.
- **Google journal prompts.** A ridiculous number of journal topics and personal essay topics are available to you (and your students) at the click of a mouse. One promise I can make is that, if you turn to the internet for prompts, you will never, ever run out of things to write about.

Benefits of Journaling as a Meditation Practice

You can choose to journal to develop ideas, or you can choose to journal to calm your mind as a form of meditation. If you choose the latter, the benefits are obvious and can include opportunities to:

- pause and reflect
- notice your surroundings

- slow down
- think
- clear your mind
- distinguish between the essential and the nonessential. (In other words, we don't want to write it all, so we only write what's important.)

But journaling can have even more profound and life-changing implications, depending on how you do it.

Lara Zielin, the author of *Author Your Life* and creator of the Author Your Life manifesting process, teaches her students to write about themselves as if they were characters in a piece of fiction—meaning they should refer to themselves in the third person. In the entry, the writer describes a goal or state of being they desire. Writing in the third person (he/she/they) creates a distance that allows the writer to get out of her head and see the goal as detached from the ego, thus making it more attainable.

The journal entry can be about a material goal ("Danny is excited to have just purchased his annual pass to Disneyland") or something more personal and emotional ("Danny lives a life full of joy and contentedness where abundance flows freely and peace is a daily occurrence"). Both are helpful for experiencing a more mindful and fulfilling life. Consistently writing about the life you want as if it's happening to someone else, Zielin notes, puts you in the mindset to make it happen and allows you to notice opportunities for next steps, thereby moving you closer to your goals.

A Couple Quick Exercise Ideas

What if you can't think of anything to say in your journal? That's a legitimate concern. I've heard many writers say they would journal, but then worry that they have no idea how to begin. But there are actually many ways to get started.

In an article called "Journaling as Meditation," Mind Fuel Daily suggests choosing open-ended statements that, especially if you're unsure of what to write or how to continue, can take you deeper into the topic you're writing about and how you're thinking and feeling about it. Start with a statement like, "At this moment . . . " or "I am feeling . . . " and simply explore what comes up in the next five minutes. You can also start with "I am grateful for . . . " and make journaling part of your gratitude practice.

Similarly, in *Wild Mind: Living the Writer's Life*, author Natalie Goldberg recommends a number of open-ended statements that can get you or your students going, including starting with "But what I really want to say is . . . " or, if the assignment has to do with a memory, you can use "I remember . . . "

The key is to keep writing, and whenever you start to run out of steam, simply write the open-ended starter again and riff on a new memory, new idea, or new thing to be grateful for.

Using these open-ended statements as free-write prompts in class is a great way to have your students "empty the cup" and quiet their minds so they can focus on the day's lesson.

Journaling Tips:

1. Breathe. (Thought you were going to get away without doing that, didn't you?)
2. Stay in the moment. Hide your phone and avoid distractions.
3. When your mind starts to wander (and if you're human, it will), simply come back to the original prompt and start writing again.
4. Don't let your mind edit. Just get the words down.
5. Observe and document. See what you see. Describe it. Use *all* of your senses.
6. Later, if you want to, mine the journal entry as raw material for stories, poems, or classroom assignments.

7. If you like the journaling process and you experience meditation-style benefits, be consistent. Work it into your regular schedule. Sessions don't need to be longer than 10–20 minutes.

For years, I would buy and carry a number of fancy journals, but they all seemed so nice that I was loath to spill a drop of ink on them. Since taking up bullet journaling in 2016, however, I have filled scads of journals with to-do lists, ideas, notes from online courses, poems, and various other thoughts and scribbles.

It's been helpful, sure.

But mostly it's been fun.

Danny's Writing Diary:

My Daybook

Our eighth-grade social studies teacher once asked us to start a journal. Kind of a day-to-day diary thing. But as a middle-school boy, there was no way I was going to call it a diary. And calling it my journal seemed equally unlikely. Somehow—perhaps at the suggestion of Mr. S., our teacher—the series of loose-leaf notebook pages in a manila folder became known as my "daybook." To this day, I have no idea what that means, but that's what it was called. My first entry was March 18, 1977.

Every night I sat down at the desk in my bedroom, pulled my daybook from my drawer, and documented the events of the day. I wrote about what my family did, where we went (if anywhere), and what my friends and I were up to at school. The entries were short, most not more than two or three sentences. And not being a fan of ink, I started my daybook in pencil. I wrote about such earth-shattering experiences as the Spring Fling dance, girls I had crushes on, going bowling with church friends, and the day my uncle gave me his CB radio (which, at the time, was all the rage).

The actual assignment was only supposed to last for two weeks. For some reason, though, I kept going. In the fall, I started high school and wrote about that. I wrote about my sophomore year as well. In the third year, which would have been March of 1979, I started writing in ink, and instead of starting each entry with the salutation Daybook:, I simply put the date. The amazing thing is that, when I look back now, all I have to do is read what happened on a particular day (even when there is no commentary or reflection), and all the memories and emotions come flooding back.

In retrospect, switching to ink seems like a meaningful transition. I mean, I went from the ephemeral experience of writing with a pencil to making a more indelible mark with a blue Bic Cristal Stic pen. Today, I suppose, I would be keeping these same entries here in Google Drive, where I am writing this to you today. In short, I was growing up.

Before I knew it, my junior year was in the books—literally. Then senior year: prom, graduation, and everything in between. I wrote about the plays I was in, the obligatory family adventure to the Grand Canyon, the outings with friends, and whatever was going on with my siblings, though the fun thing about my daybook is that I was the star of it, so other family members tended to have strictly supporting roles. Such is the narcissism of your average teenager.

My last entry was during my second year of community college. Why did I stop then? I'm not sure. What I noticed, upon recently reviewing the entries, is that as time wore on, I did more reflecting, added more commentary, and shared more of my feelings. The entries were longer and more introspective. So it's entirely possible that I just got lazy or tired or both. Or maybe school just took more effort and I was writing more for my classes. Or maybe I just lost interest. Hard to say. The last few entries, dated somewhere in the spring of 1982, had much to do with a young woman named Carolinn I'd met in my women's studies class. But I digress . . .

But here's the thing I'm proud of: I don't think too many people can say, at the age of fifty-nine, that they have their entire high school career documented—day by day—and that those documents are sitting on a shelf in their bedroom closet. It's always a trip to pull out those six blue three-ring binders and take a trip down memory lane. And one thing I've learned is that memory is fallible. Memories I thought happened weeks, months, and sometimes years apart were *often, in actuality, only days apart, according to the empirical evidence of my daybook. It's stunning how malleable our memories are and how easy it is to misremember something.*

As it turns out, writing in my daybook was, all things considered, an incredible writing practice. It taught me discipline, the benefits of sitting down and writing whether I wanted to or not, how small bits of writing add up, and that carefully documented details are the bricks laid into what eventually becomes an entire edifice of experience.

CHAPTER 12

BIC

Seasoned writers adhere to an important acronym: BIC.

BIC stands for "Butt in Chair."

In other words, if you are interested in getting your writing done, you must have the discipline to sit your butt down, start typing, and keep your butt in the chair for the work to happen.

This goes for you and the writing you would like to do, as well as for your students and their assignments. This may mean less Netflix bingeing, fewer video games, minimal Facebook scrolling on your smartphone, and sending out fewer tweets (oh, the horror!). Writing may not always be a choice, especially for your students, but how we write and when we write is most definitely a choice, and it works best if we make a conscious decision to create a habit where that writing is more likely to happen. Books, poems, stories, blog posts, church bulletins, and essays assigned in AP Language or US

History—none of these write themselves. Just as extended sessions of sitting on the meditation cushion often gets uncomfortable (sometimes downright painful!), we must have the discipline and passion to create these pieces of work, even when we experience discomfort.

This means committing the time, sitting down, and stringing the words together.

The good news is that I enjoy creating works of art out of words. I want to do it. I *need* to do it. So I always tell people, "If you want to write, then write. But if you don't like it or don't enjoy it, then by God, STOP writing." Life is difficult enough as it is. And make sure you are not writing for love, fame, publication, good grades, or money. Those are paths to nowhere. I hate to break it to you, but no one cares if you (or I, for that matter) write another word as long as we live.

The only *real* reason to write is because you want to and enjoy it.

But whether you're a teacher with a family and simply want to start a blog or you're a student with an upcoming essay deadline whose schedule includes violin lessons, band practice, play rehearsal, or your boyfriend's grandmother's birthday party, it can be challenging to carve out time to commit words to the page. Life responsibilities are real, and though it takes a great deal of intentionality to make the time for the activities and pastimes we wish to pursue, we must understand that our other responsibilities may sometimes impede our forward motion. We must accept that we will have various seasons of life, and our ability to produce written work may wax and wane with the rhythm of our lives. Recognizing these seasons in life is also a part of mindfulness.

While writing my last book, for example, I would set my alarm for five a.m., and when the alarm went off, I would swing my legs over the side of the bed, open my laptop, and start typing for twenty-five to thirty minutes before I got ready for work. What I noticed with this book you're reading now is that I was much older, sleepier, and crankier. The few times I tried to wake up at five a.m. and start typing for this book, I wound up peering through the slits of tired eyes, and to figure out what I wrote you would have needed a decoder ring from a 1950s cereal box.

And then I remembered how I wrote my first three novels. My daughters were young, and I would get up and get ready for work quite early (right around five a.m., in fact). After driving to work and getting settled in my classroom—cue a hot cup of black coffee and some classic rock on the boombox—I would start writing. With the book you are currently reading, I realized I could go back to that schedule. The key was that I was already completely ready for the day—I had showered, eaten breakfast, and was in my work environment. I wasn't just rolling out of bed and trying to think coherently. My brain synapses were firing a little more effectively because I was more awake. I was able to keep my butt in the chair and produce some words.

This book was written because I got up at 5:25, was in my classroom by seven a.m., and was ready to write from 7:10 to 7:40. This happened at least twice a week, but usually three or four times a week. Thirty minutes may not seem like a lot of time, and at first it didn't seem like much to me, either. But by doing it consistently, putting my butt in the chair, and continuing to type, the pages began stacking up. Then, almost before I knew it, I had a book-length manuscript sitting on the filing cabinet next to my dirty coffee mugs.

For students, keeping their butt in the chair may look like not squandering the time the teacher gives them to work in class, spending less time on social media on their phones when they get home, getting up a little bit earlier every morning, or staying up a half an hour later every night. For you, it may mean all of those things or being even more creative about how you navigate your work, family, and home responsibilities.

Whatever works.

The moral of the story is that there is always a way.

Just keep your butt in the chair.

CHAPTER 13

Rituals

When I was very young and still committed to my dream of becoming the next David Cassidy, I spent my time writing reams and reams of what I thought of as song lyrics. During each session, I would wait to get "inspired" before I would try to write anything. I would often put albums on to get in the right frame of mind to write these lyrics. The artists I would play included everyone from Michael Jackson to the Beatles to Boz Scaggs to the aforementioned member of the Partridge Family.

What I didn't realize until much later is that while inspiration is good, you can't wait around for it. Writing is a craft. It takes discipline. It takes a plan. Just like you probably tell your own students, if you want to become a better writer, you need to write. Even when you don't feel like it.

But what I did stumble upon during those days of penning verse after verse is the importance of rituals. It was a very mindful act to select a set of albums, maybe even the order I wanted to hear particular songs (in fact, I'm completely convinced that, somewhere around 1978, I single-handedly created the idea of a playlist), and use that as fuel, inspiration, and sort of a creative energy to write.

Even before I knew of things like Zen and mindfulness, I understood the importance of getting still and silent to connect with the inner source, where the words came from. I often sequestered myself in my bedroom with my notebook paper and pencil, and, after what I guess I would now call a rudimentary form of meditation—essentially, breathing and clearing my mind—I started to write. I never did become the next David Cassidy, but it's still fun to dig through the box of lyrics I wrote in seventh grade and count up exactly how many songs I penned to Cyndi or Stephanie or Joy over forty-five years ago.

If you teach writing at any level and are interested in improving (or even starting) your own writing practice, it might behoove you to create your own rituals—if only because you'll get to play around with words like *behoove*, and how fun is that? Sit down at the same time every morning, stream a certain singer or band, park yourself in front of a certain window with your favorite view, or take your laptop to your favorite coffeehouse. Whatever works for you. Creating personal rituals can't help but formalize your structure, create a sense of routine, and strengthen your discipline as a writer.

The same is true at your school when students are writing their essays about symbols in *The Scarlet Letter* or the process of photosynthesis or the impact of the Trail of Tears. Setting up writing rituals can make the writing experience more thoughtful, in-depth, and engaging.

What rituals could you create for your students before they write that would let their subconscious know that it's time to express?

Here are some suggestions:

- Do some breathing/meditating with them.
- Play some music.

- Choose a writing day. (If it's Tuesday, it must be poetry day . . .)
- Journal or free write in response to prompts every day for five minutes.
- Read a poem.
- Review previously written work.

The list is limited only by your creativity and imagination.

You've probably heard of famous writers who took a walk, had a glass of wine, or lit a candle before putting quill to parchment, the latter of which I do not recommend in the classroom unless you have a state-of-the-art fire alarm system. If you practice long enough, though, you will eventually figure out what rituals work for you, what habits and patterns unlock inspiration and give you access to the language and thoughts you and/or your students are after.

New parents often hear about the importance of bedtime rituals so that their offspring learn when it's time to sleep. Those might involve reading a bedtime story, having a bath, or singing a soothing lullaby. Your writing rituals—either at home or with your students in the classroom—are no different. When you create rituals for you or your students, you are providing a subconscious signal that it's time to write.

Danny's Writing Diary:

"Pleasure Cruise"

At the end of my sixth-grade school year, my mother had to go in to the office and speak to the administration to make sure I was going to pass and make it to middle school. I'd been shirking my schoolwork, and my fate was anything but certain.

My excuse for not completing my assignments?

I was working on my "book."

Thankfully, the administrator decided to let me move on to middle school, and during the summer between eighth and ninth grade, right before I entered the magical world of high school, I was visiting my aunt when I noticed she had a manual typewriter. I asked to borrow it.

I took that behemoth home and started clacking away. I can't remember everything I wrote, but there is one artifact left from that summer—a short story called "Pleasure Cruise."

In my writerly way, I wanted the title to be ironic because it was a detective story that concerned a jewel heist in my hometown of San Diego. Apparently, I'd recently learned the maxim "Write what you know." And just to be clear: what I knew was San Diego, not jewel heists.

Though the pages are dingy and yellowed, and the font smeared and uneven, flipping through the tattered manuscript still takes me back to my bedroom in the summer of 1977. The story is four pages long, was written in a single sitting, and, as I recall, the plot has more holes than a Swiss cheese factory.

The unindented first paragraph begins, "Off the Pacific, in San Diego, an event that would shock an entire community, yet would be held confeidential (sic) was in the process of happening."

Let's break this down:

1. *In addition to "Write what you know," I clearly had also recently learned about grabbing the reader's attention by writing a hook.*
2. *Though a gallant effort at sentence variety, this is quite possibly the most awkward syntax known to humankind.*
3. *Most embarrassing, in retrospect, is the notion that something could "shock" an entire community if it was being "held confidential." What was I even thinking? It simply does not make sense.*

Other unforgettable lines include:

- *Mr. Gregory T. Roper the millionaire convientally (sic) had a board meeting for the oil company he was president of. One fact that would never leave that meeting room was that Mr. Roper never showed.*
- *Detective Hammond left the harbor at nine o'clock Monday morning with one bad vendetta.*
- *If either had known what the other had planned, they would both have been in frenzies.*
- *What mattered most is that the old hut and the shrunken heads on the island meant that someone else was on the island, not only Roper. Not only Hammond. But who? A witch doctor? Cannibals? Maybe the shrunken heads weren't real. But then maybe they were.*

Practicing my mystery and suspense skills seemed to be the order of the day in this story, but my gripping tale would hardly have had Tom Clancy and David Baldacci quaking in their boots.

Oh, and in case you're riveted and on the edge of your seat, the story ends with Roper, the jewel thief, completely disappearing into thin air, Detective Hammond going insane and being committed to an institution, and the mysterious island just off the coast of San Diego bursting into flames.

"Pleasure Cruise" had a better ending than my "Super" story, but that's like saying Twilight *is more poetic than* 50 Shades of Grey.

CHAPTER 14

Paying Attention

Filmmaker Stanley Kubrick once said, "Observation is a dying art." I don't completely disagree, but I don't think it's so much that observation is dying as that it's on life support. So many entertainment options exist in our world, and the graphics and CGI of those entertainments are so realistic and powerful that, in many ways, we have stopped seeing with our own eyes and using our own senses to notice and document specific details that come from our own experience. Instead, it gets easy to get lazy, and we give up the responsibility to observe and hand it over to artists like Kubrick, who are often more than happy to do the seeing for us. It goes without saying, of course, that Kubrick, director of such cinematic masterpieces as *2001: A Space Odyssey*, *A Clockwork Orange*, and *The Shining*, clearly knows a thing or two about how to render a specific detail in a telling and evocative way. So we leave our imaginations up to the

Stanley Kubricks, Steven Spielbergs, Spike Lees, and Jane Campions of the world.

As writers, however, neither you nor your students have that luxury. If you want to reach next-level writing, you must relearn how to observe, see, and pay attention to the world around you.

I've always been grateful that, fortunately, I was taught this from an early age. When I was very young, my parents often drove us to a local drugstore called Thrifty's to get ice cream. With a single income and four kids, there wasn't always a lot of money for entertainment, and at Thrifty's, you could get one scoop for a nickel, two for a dime, and three for fifteen cents. This was a long time ago, of course. When our parents could afford a triple for all six of us, we knew it had been a good month.

After buying the ice cream, our family would retire to the car where we would enjoy our treats (French vanilla, in my case), but it was what would happen next that informed my observational skills for the rest of my life. Having very little money for expensive entertainment, my family would sit in the car and people watch.

What does that mean, exactly?

Well, a few things.

We might comment on someone's loud shirt or fancy moustache or wacky hairdo. We might talk smack about a group of hooligan-looking kids. We might make fun of the barefoot hippies smoking by the Firestone tire shop at the end of the strip mall (this was the midseventies, after all). I also remember how my father, ever the jokester, would vocally re-create the rhythm of a person's gait. (Someone with a lumbering gait might get, for example, "buh-dump, buh-dump, buh-dump.")

Was this mean? Probably. Possibly. I don't know. But I do know that I don't think my family ever meant it that way, and it was long before the term "political correctness" was ever coined, so I don't know if we even thought of such things. Plus, it goes without saying that at the age of ten I found it absolutely hilarious.

In the end, we were all just fascinated with people, and one of the reasons that I gravitated toward acting and writing fiction is that those ice-cream-eating, people-watching sessions created a lifelong curiosity in me about who people are and why they do what they do.

If you ask any decent actor or writer, they will tell you the same thing: it pays to watch people and isolate and re-create specific details, habits, and behavior. It permits the artist to create characters that are more real and believable. It allows the artist to understand and appreciate elements of the world that other people ignore. Despite my family's potential insensitivities, our noticing people was a way of connecting to others, and ultimately it created empathy and compassion in us. Good writers, of course, employ this empathy as they compose their drafts to create specificity and detail in their writing.

Furthermore, observation—this idea of paying attention—is the intersection between writing and mindfulness because it's where you stop and notice. It's where you find the details. It's where you get specific. In our current world, we hardly ever take the time to stop and notice what's around us. We don't focus on specific details. We don't notice colors, textures, shapes, or patterns. Beyond how much this will improve your writing, the upshot of observation is that we learn to take an interest in what is going on in our world, we learn to document our experiences, and we learn to appreciate the depth of our existence.

When being awarded the Peace Prize of the German Book Trade, writer Susan Sontag (who has been known to have some pretty good Zen in her own pen), said, "A writer, I think, is someone who pays attention to the world." During another time of reflection, she noted that, "It's all about paying attention. Attention is vitality. It connects you with others. It makes you eager. Stay eager."

Even those things that you think are "familiar"—your home, your neighborhood, your classroom—can be seen in a new light if you go about it the right way. In my book *The Zen Teacher*, I talk about a quote by Heraclitus, who said, "You can't step twice into the same stream."

It might be easy to think, "This is so boring. I'm always here. What could be new about THIS?"

But the idea is that—even though it seems to be the same stream—every time you step into it, the *world* is different, *you* are different, and yes, even the *space* is difference. Ergo, your *experience* can be different, and, if you're lucky, it can be more interesting, intriguing, and/or entertaining, even when you're splashing around in the same stream.

It's easy to assume that because we've spent so much time in our houses and yards, our living and dining rooms, and our bedrooms and family rooms, there is nothing new to see.

But it doesn't have to be that way.

There's plenty to see—if you know how to look for it.

What if, for example, you chose to open blinds that were usually closed, peek into a closet, dig through the junk drawer, explore the garage, sit under your apple tree in the backyard, grab an old book off the bookshelf and sit and read it, or . . . well, you get the idea.

You might find the keys you were looking for, discover an ingredient in the back of the pantry for those cookies you love to make (and now have time to bake), unearth a board game you forgot you had, or any number of other surprises.

There *is* a way to find the new in the old.

Here's how you can re-engage with the familiar, so that you can write from a place of your own attention:

1. Stop.
2. Breathe (always breathe).
3. Tune in to your senses.
4. Look around.
5. What do you notice about the room that you haven't noticed before? What do you hear? What do you smell? What do you taste? (Maybe this last one is for the kitchen, but I don't judge!)
6. Identify one detail, one object, one space that you typically don't acknowledge or notice.
7. What is special, different, or interesting about that detail, object, or space?

8. How can you interact or engage with it in a new way?
9. How many new experiences can you notice, count, and document in your "familiar" space?

Intentionally paying attention, especially in places that seem "familiar" or "typical," will, quite simply, improve your writing.

Here's what I say on pages 78–79 of *The Zen Teacher* about Heraclitus's quote:

> Even when I read this quote for the first time, the meaning behind it took my breath away. Instantly, I knew how much I'd been taking for granted, how much I had failed to see, to realize, to know. As if a light switch had flipped, I suddenly saw how routine and mundane my days had become by assuming that, merely because I've been somewhere before, there couldn't possibly be anything new to experience.
>
> I was wrong...
>
> Even as I write this at my desk [in my classroom] and take a break to go outside, I see the way the afternoon sunlight falls at a slant on the building across the grass, I watch the leaves' shadows dance on the sidewalk, and I hear students' laughter echoing in the hallways.
>
> Every time I step out, I see something new.

Same stream. New experience.

Beloved poet Mary Oliver says, "To pay attention, this is our endless and proper work."

Ask yourself: What am I taking for granted in this space?

How can I experience it in a new and fresh way?

In what way can I explore it more deeply and thoroughly?

How can I get to *know* it better?

Never underestimate the power of observation, of noticing, of paying attention to details.

Pay attention and it will, quite simply, pay you back.

CHAPTER 15

White Space

Short sentences, short paragraphs, short pages, and entire short chapters are okay.

Don't be afraid of white space on the page.

Danny's Writing Diary:

Published Poet

Writer's Market, *a tome thicker than a Bible, serves as a directory for writers looking to publish their work. In the old days,* Writer's Market *even had a tiny section for poetry. They may still.*

And that's how I found myself in my best friend's house in 1977, cranking out three poems on his mother's manual typewriter and trying to figure out submission guidelines. (Thirteen-year-old me had no idea, for example, what "SASE" stood for.) After poring over the poetry section of Writer's Market *in the public library—even then, a copy cost almost thirty dollars, and that was far above my budget for a book that didn't even have any pictures—I finally settled on a potential market, a magazine called* Modern Bride.

I copied down all of the pertinent information in my notebook.

Had I ever seen the publication?

Of course not.

All I knew was that I wrote love poetry, and modern brides were in love.

Synchronicity.

The thing is, when that inevitable rejection slip came back in the mail two or three months later, I treated it like a talisman. I treasured it, and that wisp of paper spent years in the drawer where I kept super important papers. It made me feel like a writer.

Eventually I got better at the submission process. I kept a record of my submission efforts on 3x5 index cards—alphabetized, of course.

Each one included the publication name, address, the date I submitted my work, and the date I received a response. There was also a place for comments in case I needed to take any notes.

I kept these index cards on my desk in one of those plastic recipe boxes your aunt used to have so she knew how to make the sweet potato casserole at Thanksgiving.

One of these submissions was to a little publication called Proof Rock. I knew most of these publications were labors of love for the editors, who often produced them from home, often from the kitchen table or garage—long before personal computers and desktop publishing came along. I didn't mind, though, because I was intoxicated by the idea of seeing my work in print and having a copy for myself. Submitting, keeping track of my submissions, and seeing the telltale self-addressed stamped envelope in my mailbox always meant possibility. Every time I walked to the mailbox, I wondered if this would be the time I opened up the envelope and pulled out an acceptance letter.

But when my three-poem packet came back from Proof Rock, there was a handwritten note from the editor, and she said that one of my poems had almost made it. I knew intuitively that I had reached a new level in the submission hierarchy: the personalized rejection note. I was on cloud nine for days. When I put together another batch of poems together for Proof Rock, I told the editor that I included the earlier poem again just so she could take another look since she had mentioned liking it in her previous note.

Not too long after, I heard that Writer's Market was branching out and creating a volume strictly for poetry called—creatively enough—Poet's Market.

Months later, after I had saved my pennies, I was on the phone with the bookstore asking if they had a copy of Poet's Market. While I was on hold, my sister came in with the mail and handed me the packet from Proof Rock. When I opened it up, there was a note from the editor saying she had accepted the original poem she liked and would be publishing it. I'm sure I surprised the bookstore clerk with my *wild ramblings about the irony of being on the phone asking about Poet's Market when I'd just gotten the news that my very first poem was being published. I'm sure if I had been in the store, she would have called security.*

Several months later, my copy of Proof Rock *came in the mail, and there was my poem for all the world to see. The journal itself was saddle-stapled, had a card-stock cover, and consisted of a group of poems that had clearly been typed on a typewriter, after which the pages had been Xeroxed. But the quality of the publication didn't matter to me at all. Other people were finally going to see my poetry. To me, it was as profound as the Dead Sea Scrolls, the Magna Carta, or Bob Dylan's* Tarantula.

My writing mattered.

My ideas were being disseminated.

I was hooked. Turning the page and seeing my poem with my name printed at the bottom was one of the greatest things I'd ever seen.

I submitted poems for nearly a decade (1987–1997) and had nearly thirty poems published—both print and online—in journals from all over the world.

I don't submit poetry anymore, but I will say this: sending out my work, receiving the acceptance letter, and then seeing my poetry in print (either in a journal or on an attractively produced website) has been one of the profound joys of my life.

Drafting Assignments

For the next piece you write or assign to your students, simply ask:

1. "How should THIS one go?" and

2. "What does THIS piece of writing need?"

3. Pick five random topics (holidays, hobbies, describe a relative, etc.). Set a timer for ten minutes. Write for a few minutes about each topic. When the timer goes off, choose one that was going well and continue. This assignment is good writing practice for you *and* your students.

4. Take a short morning or afternoon trip to someplace where people congregate (a theme park, the beach boardwalk, a county fair, a ballgame, etc.) and spend some time just observing people. How do they move? What do they say? How do they interact? What do they seem to be focused on? Take copious notes. When you get home, write up a character sketch of one or two of the most interesting characters you encountered. Or, if you're feeling brave and frisky, write a short piece of fiction showing those two characters interacting. For an advanced move, include conflict and resolution. The drafting of these pieces will help you build the writing muscle so that you are more confident and skilled in future moments of composition.

Blank Pages and Disappointments

CHAPTER 16

Lovingkindness

The term "lovingkindness" refers to the practice of approaching life with a sense of empathy, compassion, and love. There may be nothing more worthy of the gift of lovingkindness than the world of art. Artists often have a challenging path. They put themselves out there every day and face judgment for ideas, concepts, and works of art that might be misunderstood, ignored, or, in some cases, outright rejected. This is not an easy road. Therefore, extending kindness to the people in this world is imperative.

I've only taken two creative writing classes in my life, and one took place at San Diego State University in the spring of 1984. We wrote many pieces for the class, including several short stories. But what I really remember was a packet of poems we turned in. It's not an exaggeration to say (and I have told my own students this many times) that poetry heals. Consequently, I took this assignment very seriously.

When the time came, I turned in my packet of five or six poems that I had written with great care and revised many times. A week or so later, the pack was returned.

Now, as a seasoned writer even then, I knew that feedback was beneficial. I was not afraid of critique. In fact, I was always disappointed when I received a piece of writing back from a peer editor and all they said was "Great job." That was not nearly enough for me. I genuinely wanted to know how to get better. But I was unprepared for the biting criticism I received between the lines of those poems. Judging from her comments, the instructor really seemed to think I had dashed them off and not tried very hard.

The one comment that specifically stung me was on one of my favorite poems in the packet. It said simply, "This seems like a real poem."

This seems like a real poem.

Really?

In one short sentence, this teacher—whose job it was to nurture and encourage young writers—was able to dismiss and undermine all the effort I'd put into the poem and make it seem as if, almost by accident, I had approached something resembling a "real" poem. Fortunately, I had enough self-esteem and enough confidence in my writing style to know that that comment had more to do with her (and her perception of me) than it did with anything I had written. Or, if I want to practice kindness and empathy myself, maybe she had something going on in her life and was in a bad mood when she read my work, or maybe she just dashed off the comment because she had a stack of writing waiting on the kitchen counter, and she didn't give it a second thought (I am often guilty of that myself). It could have been any of those things.

But clearly, this judgment and dismissal stayed with me because here we are thirty-six years later, and much like Mrs. Theroux's note on my "Super" story over a decade earlier, I still remember the note verbatim.

One thing I try to take away from that experience is that, regardless of how I view the "quality" of a piece of writing—a poem, for example—just by virtue of the fact that one of my students has written it, it is very much a "real" poem. If the poem exists, it's a "real" poem. And regardless of whatever thoughtless critique I may scribble on a student's paper, nothing will change that.

One form lovingkindness can take is avoiding negative self-talk. We all have that self-editor who talks trash to us as we write.

What makes you think you can write?

Who's going to want to read this crap?

This paragraph sucks.

Sound familiar?

It sure does to me.

But you know what the answer is?

Keep writing.

Just. Keep. Writing.

Tell that voice to buzz off.

I'm thinking of a different word, but we'll go with *buzz*.

That negative self-talk helps no one.

And it certainly doesn't help whatever piece of writing you're working on.

The antidote is to keep typing.

No matter what.

Then go back and make it happen again.

In *Bird by Bird*, Anne Lamott talks about what she calls "Station KFKD": that looping internal monologue that keeps telling you everything you write is terrible, that no one will ever read it, that you might as well give up because every word you put on the page is rubbish. She says that when that internal monologue is blaring, "we need to sit there, and breathe, calm ourselves down, push back our sleeves, and begin again." And I agree. But I also believe there is only one way to switch off Station KFKD, and the approach is twofold: 1) First and foremost, keep writing. The only way to get better is to keep typing. 2) Stop caring what anyone else says about what you write. Neither approach is easy, but they're crucial.

Find people who gravitate to your message, your style, and your personal charisma. In the case of your students, you are of course their default audience; they don't have the luxury of choosing a reader they know will connect with their work. So the more you can get their writing in front of an authentic audience, the better. As their writing teacher, you also realize, I'm sure, that they have extraordinarily well-developed internal monologues in their own noggins telling them precisely why a piece of writing will not work and why they are ill-equipped to make it happen. When that occurs, your job is to give them confidence and encourage them to try anyway. Your job is to instill in them the assurance that they *can* do it and that it will turn out all right, even if they don't get the grade they're hoping for. It's important that you teach them that writing is a continuum, and any one piece is not the be-all and end-all but part of the process of them simply learning how to write better.

Still, as someone who writes yourself, you know that sometimes a writer finds herself just sitting there staring at the blank page, overwhelmed and full of anxiety because the words just aren't coming.

When this happens, it is important to:

- **Be kind to yourself.** If you're not going to be kind to yourself, who is? It pays no dividends to emotionally beat up someone you love. (That's you, by the way.) Know that you have the option of showing yourself grace and forgiveness or buoying yourself up or inspiring yourself. Show yourself compassion.
- **Be kind to your students.** Not everyone is a writer. And that's okay. Some students are better at math, science, singing, woodworking, or whatever. When you see a student struggling, understand that the student sitting in front of you has many gifts, but feeling at ease with writing may not be one of them. If they can't recall a concept, this is not the time to say through gritted teeth, "What's wrong with you? I've told you this a million times." There may have been some reason, completely unbeknownst to you, as to why that student missed

that information. Of course, it may also be because they had a pair of earbuds stuck in their ears and the information had a hard time getting into their gray matter.

But in the end, does it really matter?

Grace is always the best approach.

- **Trust yourself.** It is important to learn how to trust your effort, your style, your craft. Teach your students to trust their effort and training as well. If you are earnest and have been paying attention and practicing in good faith, most of what you need will return to you if you keep breathing, stay still, and listen.

This, by the way, is true about most everything in life.

CHAPTER 17

Writer's Block

*L*ike most writers, you or your students have probably reached that unenviable moment when, whether you're on page 1 or 101, you find yourself staring at the blank page and the words just aren't coming.

You have no ideas.

You don't know what to say.

Your fingers hover over the keyboard, paralyzed, unable to construct even the simplest of sentences.

"It's not my fault," you tell yourself, instantly defensive. "I have writer's block."

And then you envision yourself in the spire of some Victorian castle in England in a dark cloak with a scarf thrown around your neck, as you sit at a tiny table where a tapered candle is flickering in the darkness, a violent thunderstorm raging outside.

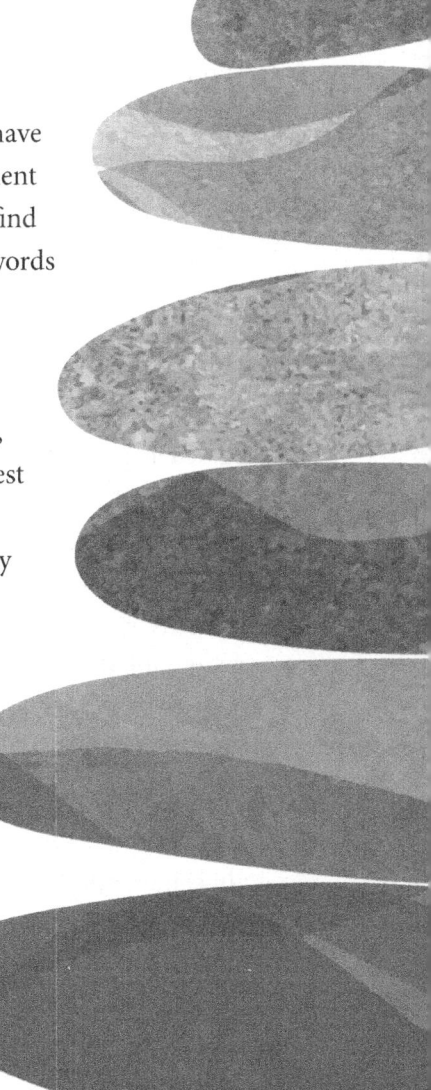

And then your hands begin to shake, and a bead of sweat forms on your upper lip.

You start looking around nervously.

Then, before you even know what's happening, you're scrubbing the baseboards in the bathroom with a toothbrush.

Anything to tamp down the guilt and shame over not sitting your butt in the chair and cranking out the words.

Ready for some tough love?

There's no such thing as writer's block.

It doesn't exist.

It's not a thing.

I understand that this is a controversial opinion. I understand that others will disagree.

But that doesn't make it not true.

Natalie Goldberg, author of *Writing Down the Bones: Freeing the Writer Within*, once said, "You are free to write the worst junk in America." I agree with her. In fact, what you can't see right now is that here I am doing just that in this first draft, just to meet my five-hundred-word quota for the day.

But that liberation, that freedom to write complete junk is what helps writers get past the keyboard paralysis.

You can't leave it like that, of course. That would be like going to church with bedhead, slippers, and a toothbrush hanging out of your mouth. You are obligated to dress it up just the tiniest little bit. (Note: A few sentences ago, I called what I was writing here "junk," and it was at first, but naturally, I later went back and tried to make it better.)

But some writers, once they decide they can't write any more, simply stop.

For some reason, many writers think they have the luxury of stalling and not doing the work.

In some ways, it's a form of vanity. Look at it this way: The plumber doesn't get plumber's block. The car mechanic doesn't get mechanic's block. And you might be thinking, "Yeah, but you don't get it. They are dealing with sinks and carburetors, and I am dealing with *ideas*."

It reminds me of a time when my friend Mike came over to help fix my toilet. He flipped houses for a living and unlike me, was extremely handy. When Mike finished fixing the toilet, I was extremely grateful and appreciative, especially considering my biggest contribution to the project was emotional support and cheerleading from the sidelines. Being humble, Mike deflected the praise.

"It's no big deal," he said. "I could never do what you do. Teaching all them kids."

"Nah," I said. "What you do is pretty damned important. The world can live without commas. Try going two days without a toilet."

Writing, as it turns out, is an art *and* a craft. It's magical when it works well, and that's the art. But when it isn't working in a magical, supernatural way, you must rely on training, experience, and the tools of your craft. When I was a journalist, you had to crank it out and meet your deadline. End of story. It might not have been great, but it was done. If your piece wasn't on the editor's desk by the deadline, the editor didn't care that you weren't "inspired." You weren't being paid to be inspired; you were being paid to write.

So why won't the words come?

What's really going on when you think you're experiencing writer's block?

Here are some possibilities.

Fear or anxiety. I was in the middle of writing this book when the coronavirus pandemic struck in March of 2020. I had been making good progress, but then I totally stalled. I was lethargic, unmotivated, and feeling a tremendous amount of anxiety about world events. Consequently, my writing progress stalled, and I couldn't think of anything to say. Just sitting down to type seemed like a major endeavor, and I didn't have a thought in my head. But in the end, I worked out what my issues were by planting my butt in the chair and typing anyway.

Make no mistake: the words sucked. But hopefully now—after miles of editing—they suck less.

Procrastination. Writing is hard. Sometimes even the most seasoned writer would rather do anything but wrangle words together: build a treehouse, clean out the garage, alphabetize the spice rack—whatever. The looming specter of the unfinished poem or story or essay or book is daunting, and we think that if we can't finish the whole thing, why even bother? So we put it off. But sitting down mindfully, taking a breath, and starting to type—regardless of the quality or purpose—is one hedge against procrastination and will help us find the words we're longing for.

Perfectionism. We all fall victim to the lure of perfectionism from time to time, but it's critical that we don't let it paralyze us. It may seem as if perfectionism comes from wanting to do our best or create something flawless. But it doesn't. It comes from fear. It comes from that place where we are afraid of what will happen if we put something out in the world and it's not accepted. We erroneously believe that if it's "perfect" (spoiler alert: there's no such thing) that it will be well received, that we won't be criticized. But be forewarned: it will *never* be perfect. So you might as well do your writing and get it done. Any time you put something out into the world, there will be armchair trolls who will roll up their sleeves just to knock you down. These are demons we creative types must learn to live with. Be in the moment, and just do the thing. As they say in the business world, "done is better than perfect."

Complacency. If we don't have to write, it's easy to give up when the words don't come. It gets easy to say "whatever" when we're writing things on spec and no one is expecting a finished piece. When we're typing for fun or just for ourselves, we are more likely to give up when we hit a wall. We are also more likely to accept substandard writing when we don't care about the outcome. How many times have you seen a student turn in a poor piece of writing (typically a dashed-off first draft), shrug, and say, "At least I turned it in." Complacency kills good writing faster than anything.

A problem with structure or plot. It's okay to be stuck. In any creative endeavor there are times when the way forward is foggy, and we aren't sure which way to turn. There are times when we've made an error, haven't planned enough, have faulty structure, or have figuratively painted ourselves into a proverbial corner. That's normal. What's not "normal" is blaming one of those issues for your so-called "writer's block." Call it what it is—an error, a structural or foundational problem, a misstep. Then fix it. But don't call it writer's block. I guarantee you that once you identify the problem and address it, the words will start flowing like water through a dike whose little Dutch boy has gone on a three-day bender in the Bahamas.

The tank might be empty. Output is related to input. So maybe you need to read more. Take a break and write something else. Go out in nature. Visit the local museum and look at some art. Watch some bad television so you know what *not* to do. It's imperative that, at least every now and then, you are filling your creative tank with inspiration from which to draw for your own artistic and creative pursuits. If you're tired, spent, exhausted, or used up creatively, you don't have the fuel necessary to put in the effort to create your thing. Creation is hard, y'all. It takes effort and energy. Effort and energy that might be depleted if you have a thousand other obligations that are using you up. Be where you are and be present. Listen to your body and what it needs. If you can't write, take some time and try filling the tank.

Here are three approaches for dealing with what you *think* is writer's block:

Write through it. When we go on a road trip, it's a marathon, not a sprint. That means that there can often be long stretches that are frustrating, boring, flat, desolate, and unremarkable. Or all of the above. But eventually, with a little patience, a few giant yawns, a few bags of Doritos, and some Pepsi, you'll reach your destination. The same is true with writing—especially with longer-form projects, such as novels. Whenever the writing starts to drag, or feels like it has stopped altogether, just keep typing. Keep your foot on the pedal and just keep slinging the words, and eventually you will make it through. It may still be desolate and flat, but you can always fix that later (see the revision section for more).

Give yourself permission to write crap. On a related note, remember that sometimes the words will be terrible, and that's okay. I understand that you want to create scenes as vivid and horrific as Stephen King's, share seven habits that are as effective as Stephen Covey's, or string together words in as beautiful and lyrical an order as Toni Morrison or Barbara Kingsolver. But allow me to let you in on a little secret: The words of those authors did not come out that way the first time through. In most cases, it took a massive amount of revision to get the writing just so. I'm willing to bet that the first drafts of those authors' work are plenty bad in many or most parts and need a ton of rewriting. In fact, in an early version of Stephen King's novel *The Shining*, the family wasn't staying in the Overlook Hotel in the Rocky Mountains but in a Super 8 hotel near the freeway in Modesto, near a 7-Eleven with an empty Redbox. I'm kidding, of course, but you get my point. As one of my business heroes, Seth Godin, says in a blog post called, "The Simple Cure for Writer's Block," "The best way to deal with it is to write, and to realize that your bad writing isn't fatal."

In other words: if you write crap, no one's gonna die.

Well, maybe, if you're writing *The Shining*, someone might, but usually, no.

Ask yourself questions. When my students tell me they are struggling with what to write—especially when it comes to their own commentary—I always tell them, first of all, that it's because they are fourteen or fifteen and no one has ever asked them what they think. Up to that point in their education, they have only ever been asked, generally speaking, to regurgitate information. But now, I tell them, we're going to explore what your thoughts and ideas are and write them down. Then I see them close their eyes and scrunch up their eyebrows. Their faces redden, and then they relax their muscles and shrug. They look at me like, "I got nothin.'" Sometimes they even say that. At that point, I tell them that if it hurts their brain at first to do it, that just means that, much like going to the gym, they're doing it correctly. Writing is a muscle they're going to strengthen as they do it more often. And when they say, "But how do I write down what I think when I don't know what I think?" that's when I say, "Ask questions."

When a student gets stuck when they're asked to write down what they think—that is to say, when they're working on commentary, an analysis, an explication, or an explanation—I encourage them to ask themselves questions:

- Why is this important?
- What does it mean?
- What is the author trying to say?
- Why did the character *do* that?
- How does the character feel?
- What have I experienced that this reminds me of?
- What am I really trying to say here?

A teacher friend of mine once wrote a list of 143 questions that students could ask themselves about a piece of literature that would jump-start their thought process, get them thinking, and give them raw material for the analysis part of their essays. As many teachers (and a truckload of empirical research the size of Rhode Island) will tell you, asking yourself questions to get at what you truly want to say is a gift you give yourself as a writer. And mindfully speaking, there is no better time to ask those questions than in the middle of the writing when you're not sure where to go.

Your students won't believe this, but you can tell them that not only is there no such thing as writer's block, but even if their grade goes down, they've made progress because they've shared their thoughts in written form, and not everyone knows how to do that. Or even cares enough to try. But they did it. They committed their thoughts to paper. And that's one of the most powerful things I know.

The funny thing is: once I have an idea of where I'm going, and I get lost in the flow of creation, writing feels pretty damned good. In fact, it's bliss. There are worse ways to spend one's time: I am sharing my ideas and clarifying what I think, not merely whiling away the hours playing *Mario Kart*, watching *The Bachelorette*, or reading the comments by trolls on political articles on the internet.

Not only am I doing something worthwhile, but at the end of it, I have something to show for it.

In the end, there's only writing, stringing words and sentences together in an attempt to inform or move or persuade or entertain.

The key is to keep typing until you get past the crap and you reach the parts that shine.

Danny's Writing Diary:

The All-You-Can-Drink Beverage Bar

In the late eighties, I spent two and a half years in Los Angeles pursuing acting. I had just finished college with a bachelor's degree in drama, and I lived in San Diego, so giving LA a shot was almost a no-brainer. I will never regret my decision, but there were two moments during my sojourn in the City of Angels that caused a seismic shift in my perspective, two moments that taught me that my time as an actor was over.

The first is that I went back into teaching. The trick for all actor wannabes is to find a job that also allows time off to go to auditions. Substitute teaching was perfect. If I had an audition, I just didn't accept a sub call that day. Before that, I made my living in Los Angeles working in offices, typing letters and answering phones. But what I wasn't expecting was that when I went back into teaching, I found myself saying, "This is what I love, and I feel like I'm making a difference, so why am I not doing this at home?" Less than three months later, I was back in San Diego looking for a teaching position.

But the other moment where I knew my acting pursuits had come to an end—the one that has to do with writing—concerns an audition I went to one Saturday afternoon.

The audition was for a play being produced at a small theater in the middle of Hollywood. Like many theaters, this particular space had a stage door in the alley behind the theater building, which is where the auditioning actors were asked to wait. As it sat in the middle of a bustling city, it was noisy, dirty, and more than a little stinky. Nevertheless, I patiently waited my turn with the other acting hopefuls.

It soon became clear, though, that the producers were falling behind, and the afternoon dragged on.

Around four or five in the afternoon, I said to myself, "If you leave now, you can make it to Carl's Jr. and get some writing done before you need to be home."

In recent weeks, I had been going to the nearby Carl's Jr., which was only a mile or so from my apartment, getting a soda, and writing poetry in my poetry notebook. The thing is, I was in starving-artist mode, and they had an all-you-can-drink beverage bar. For around a dollar, I could buy a soda (and maybe add some fries when I was super flush), and then I could bust out my notebook and write for hours. And I mean hours. I used to think of it as "The Poor Man's Writers Retreat."

Before you could say "Al Pacino," I had made it back to my car from that noisy, smelly alleyway, and I was on my way to Carl's Jr.

It was probably a month or so later, right around the time I went back into substitute teaching, when I realized I'd reached a turning point in my acting career. And by "turning point," I mean the end of it.

I had to admit to myself that if I wasn't willing to persevere in that alleyway when the producers were running behind, when there was no telling when or if I would get my turn, when each audition I walked away from might have been a step on the way to my big break, then maybe I just wasn't committed enough to my dream of being an actor.

In that moment, I made a choice.

I chose writing over acting.

Not too long after that moment in the alley, I chose teaching over acting.

So I had to accept that maybe, just maybe there was another path for me.

But there was something else that I could not ignore.

I had to admit to myself that teaching fed my professional soul so much more than typing letters and answering phones in someone else's business. And poetry fed my creative soul even more than acting.

So I started thinking to myself that if I was brave enough, I would move back home and go back to teaching and focus on just becoming a poet.

And if there is a job more thankless or uncertain than journeyman actor, it's poet.

But teaching was my calling.

And writing—poetry, in particular—was my jam.

It was the right decision.

I've never looked back.

CHAPTER 18

Intuition

How do you know when a piece is done?
You don't.

You make a choice, and then you make a commitment.

As a famous painter once said, "It's not so much that I finish a painting, but that I abandon it."

But while you may struggle to decide if you've done enough revision, editing, and polishing, you do have one mindful tool at your disposal to help you decide.

That tool is your intuition.

Intuition is that small, quiet voice inside us that tells us what to do and which way to go. Some people call it a hunch or a gut feeling. But it's more than that. Sometimes it borders on the spiritual. It's been my experience (and science backs this up) that our intuition is (a) usually right and (b) wants to help. It's in our best interest, then, to pay attention. We need to learn to trust what that voice is telling us. It's also worth mentioning that part of mindfulness is being able to be still and listen to what's going on inside you.

Seasoned writers—in fact, artists of all experience levels—understand the profound importance of being still and listening to the guidance that comes from the subconscious. They know, intuitively, that plowing forward isn't always the best approach.

Can you, with effort, make your writing better with subsequent drafts?

Of course.

Will that work with endless drafts and endless revisions?

Not hardly. There is most definitely a law of diminishing returns. As it turns out, by not listening to your intuition, you can actually damage the piece. You have to find the middle ground. The sweet spot.

It will never be *perfect*.

But at some point, it has to be *done*.

And the best way to figure out if it's done is to get quiet and listen to your intuition.

Like most artists, I am never finished with the final version of whatever I'm working on, but rather, at some point I must decide it's time to simply stop. It doesn't matter how many revisions I've done or how many revisions I think it still might be able to withstand; sometimes it's good to realize that the project just isn't going to get any better.

We need to let our students know this, too. Even after working with them on an essay or a poem or any other piece of writing, we need to show them that sometimes we've done the best we can and we need to move on to the next writing challenge where, presumably, we will have improved our skills via practice, and the next piece will go slightly better. We need to allow ourselves as teachers (and them as students) to look at their writing and say, "Enough."

"How long should a short story be?" the old question asks. The old (and admittedly cryptic) answer is always "As long as the story needs to be." And I totally get it. Once the little voice inside you decides that you're done and that you've reached the end, stop typing. Also, listen to your characters and where they say they need to go. Don't force them to go where they don't want to go. If you're quiet enough, still enough to listen, they will tell you. One of the best parts of writing fiction is that, when you're in the groove and feeling that amazing state called "flow," the characters will almost take over and act on their own. What fiction writer doesn't love that?

But what about nonfiction? How does intuition work there? When tapping into your inner voice for expository writing, consider this: Is it a topic that will resonate with people? Is there a market for it? For students, will my teacher be interested in it and look favorably on it?

Listen to your gut.

Many years ago I decided to write a middle grade chapter book. I had several unpublished novels under my belt, which meant that the manuscripts were languishing in a file cabinet drawer in my classroom office. I felt the idea was a good one. In fact, I saw potential for a series (think: *Diary of a Wimpy Kid*), and in my ignorance, I thought, "I can knock this out in no time. How hard can this be?" After getting about forty pages in, however, I realized that I had no business writing that particular book. I had no experience. As it turned out, a middle grade chapter book was simply not in my wheelhouse.

I could have soldiered on and finished the manuscript—and I may have even learned a few things about writing—but something was telling me to stop. A little voice deep inside tapped me on the shoulder and said quietly, "This is not for you."

Because I listened to that little voice, I was able to move on and write other pieces that made a difference—both in my life and in the lives of others.

CHAPTER 19

Writing Is a Continuum

A friend of mine, who happened to be a member of our English department, came into my classroom one lunch period visibly upset. She was also a writer and several years before had been fortunate enough to land a three-book contract for a young adult series. The books had been out for years at that point, but she was upset that afternoon because her agent had just informed her that the first of the novels in the series had been "remaindered."

A book is "remaindered" when it stops selling well and the publisher attempts to liquidate the existing stock by slashing the cover price. Since my books have not been published by a major publisher, I have never been in that situation, but I certainly understand how humbling that experience might be for a writer. My heart went out to her in that moment, and I tried to offer what support I could.

During our conversation, I hit on a philosophy that I hope helped her a little bit and that I've kept tucked in my back pocket for the many years since then because it always gives me a great deal of perspective no matter what is going on with my own writing.

What my friend and I learned that day is that writing is a continuum. Nothing you or your students do is ever about a single piece, a single project, essay, article, or book. Fundamentally, it's about the process and the joy you get out of the doing of the thing. It's about the liberating bliss of knitting words, sentences, images, and ideas together that create not only new thought but, in many cases, entirely new worlds.

That lunch conversation with my good friend was over a decade ago, but I remember it vividly because of how much she taught me. I was able to live vicariously through her experience of grief and disappointment, and yet it gave us both a reminder that while hearing about the remaindered book was, indeed, quite a sad moment in an otherwise accomplished literary career (and a definite bump in the writing road, for sure), it also was a powerful reminder that she still had many more stories inside her that she would, over time, commit to paper and use to inform and entertain audiences that she hadn't even become aware of yet.

As someone who puts pen to paper or fingers to keyboard, you may find yourself facing, from time to time, writing obstacles and misfortunes, but if you want to be absolutely in the moment with your writing and mindful of what you're putting on the page, you can't be concerned with what you've already published, who's doing the reading, the status of the last book you've written, or what your next book will be.

Your only focus should be—in fact, *must* be—on your fingers as they type the letters that form the words of your work. You must be entranced and consumed by the art you are creating as your fingers fly dexterously across the keyboard.

Why?

Because this moment is all you have, and right now, this piece of writing is all that matters.

You may publish what you've written, or you may not. You may get a hefty advance, or you may not. Meryl Streep may win an Academy Award for starring in the film adaption of your novel, or some Angelina Jolie wannabe may win a Razzie for stinking up what was a pristine work of art when it left your Google Drive.

It's all part of the process.

Furthermore, your students may get an A on this essay, or they may not. But despite their desire to graduate, it's never the letter grade that matters. What matters is the process, the continuum, the continual Zen-like practice and improvement of the doing of the thing—regardless of the outcome. So when your students have revised that essay to the *n*th degree and still aren't happy with their grade, gently remind them that even though they did not get the kudos they were hoping for, they created something that, prior to their creating it, did not exist in the world, and that, all by itself, is pretty special.

Miraculous, really.

When it comes to thinking of your students as writers, think of a time line that goes throughout their entire life (or at the very least from first to twelfth grade), and imagine each of their writing assignments falling somewhere on that timeline and getting better and better as the timeline progresses.

One of the greatest gifts you can give your students is the understanding that their personal worth is not connected to any single piece of writing and that each essay, poem, story, or free write is just a part of the continuum, just a piece of the puzzle. If this piece of writing doesn't go the way they want, there's always next time.

I have had my own disappointments in writing—a lack of publishing opportunities, "no thank yous" from agents, and enough rejection slips from literary journals to form a canoe I could christen the SS *Iowa Review*. But each time, I got up, brushed myself off, started typing, and shoved whatever had just been returned with a big fat "no" into that footlocker in my classroom cupboard.

And while I type, I'm just grateful for the Zen practice of writing. I'm grateful to get lost in the world of words, where my thoughts turn magically into people, places, things, and emotions. That would be magical enough, if that's where it ended.

But this continuum, this path has another gift to give.

Every time I sit down to type, every time I share my thoughts, I learn so much about myself and who I am. I learn about what I think and what I don't think. I learn more about my values. I learn about who I am when I am genuine and decent and who I am when I am bitter, angry, and resentful. I learn about my dreams, aspirations, fears, hopes, loves, and desires.

I get to explore it all.

No matter what I write, I benefit from the process. This would be the case even if my words never found their way into print. Sometimes it's super clear to me why Salinger disappeared after *The Catcher in the Rye* and spent the rest of his life writing for himself, never publishing another word for the world.

That's why I've kept typing most of my life.

I have trusted the path.

And my friend? Oh, she's fine. She has written and published three more books since that tearful lunch period and has just finished a screenplay for her latest published book that is being considered by film producers and winning awards at independent film festivals.

She's gonna be all right.

Danny's Writing Diary:

The Mall Street Journal

I worked my way through college tearing tickets at a movie theater at the mall called the Cinema Grossmont. It was one of the last single-house movie theaters in San Diego and one of two theaters in that particular mall. I worked there for over two and a half years and only decided it was time to go when I started my student teaching and one of my students was a girl who worked behind the snack bar. All it took was for the two of us to show up at one or two of the same afterwork parties for me to set my handwritten resignation note on the manager's desk.

Before that, however, when I still worked at the theater, I was on a break one afternoon and walking through the mall to buy a pretzel with cheese when I saw a little newsstand-style display with a stack of newspapers in it. Though I was a drama major and planned to be an actor, I also had a fairly solid journalism background, so the newspapers caught my attention.

Picking up an issue, the first thing I noticed was the title. It was called the Mall Street Journal. Okay, points for cleverness. Sitting on a nearby bench, I began flipping through it and saw stories about fashion and restaurant trends, mall happenings, and local San Diego events.

What I didn't see were movie reviews.

And for a mall that had not one but two movie theaters, this struck me as a massive oversight and a golden opportunity.

I looked at the masthead (many thanks to my high school journalism teacher, Mr. Anderson, for teaching me about mastheads and where they might show up in a paper) and noted the name of the editor, who also happened to be the general manager of the mall. The next time I had a shift at the theater during regular business hours, I marched into the mall office and asked to speak to her.

Amazingly, they let me. I may have even still been in my uniform—brown polyester blazer, tan polyester slacks, and a hideous brown tie with the Pacific Theater logo emblazoned across it. Looking back, I pray that I had the foresight to at least remove the plastic name tag.

I explained to the manager, whose name was Betsy, that I worked at the Cinema Grossmont, that I had seen the Mall Street Journal, and that, as good as it was, the thing I thought it was missing was a movie review section. I shared with her that not only did I have access to the latest movies, I had experience, having written scores of movie and play reviews for my high school and college newspapers. I was there to volunteer to write movies reviews for the Mall Street Journal. After my five-minute sales pitch, instead of calling security and having me forcibly removed from her office, she gave me the okay, shook my hand, and we set a deadline for my first piece.

I spent the next year writing reviews, which included getting free tickets to movie premieres and a myriad of merch for such eighties movies as Vision Quest, Silverado, and The Color Purple. But as it turns out, that cinema swag wasn't even the best part.

One day I walked into Betsy's office to hand in a review, and after some small talk, Betsy said, "Oh, here. This is for you" and she handed me an envelope. "It's for your last article."

Once I was outside Betsy's office, I opened the envelope and just stared at the contents dumbfoundedly.

Given her word choice, I assumed it was some kind of letter thanking me for my service and wishing me well.

But it wasn't.

It was a check for fifty dollars.

I was no math whiz, but it quickly dawned on me that for writing one article, I'd gotten paid more than I did for a week's worth of tearing tickets, filling large snack bar sodas, and cleaning up empty popcorn tubs in Theater 3.

I stood there staring at my check. Mall walkers and young moms with strollers had to maneuver around this dumb kid staring at a piece of paper in his sweaty hands.

My biggest question was: Would I buy a Swatch watch or put it toward the brand-new Nintendo gaming system?

But I kept coming back to one thought: "You can get paid for your writing."

I only got one or two more fifty-dollar checks, and whether the gig ended because the Mall Street Journal ceased publication or because I left the theater to teach, I don't recall.

But it didn't matter.

For a while, I was getting paid for something I wrote.

And if you are holding this book in your hands, it's happened again.

Four decades later.

Thank you.

Blank Pages and Disappointments Assignments

1. Remember always to approach your writing practice with a great deal of grace and self-compassion. Words and language are invaluable but imperfect vehicles for expressing our thoughts and often fall short of the mark. But that doesn't mean we shouldn't keep trying. So when it doesn't go the way you hoped, take a step back, breathe, and forgive—forgive your mind, your words, and yourself. And please keep in mind how often your students feel they have missed the mark with their written communication. Remember that they are learning (as are we all), and have compassion for them as well.

2. If the words aren't coming and you find yourself experiencing what you perceive as writer's block, try writing through it, ask yourself questions, or fill your creative tank by reading, listening to music, or viewing other types of art.

3. If you write something you feel didn't turn out very well, remember that writing is a continuum and it isn't about any one piece. You don't like this piece? Write another.

Revision

CHAPTER 20

Peer Response

We are almost always too close to our work to evaluate it objectively. Consequently, getting feedback on your writing from others is one of the most important steps in the writing process. Because humans are complex (and, frankly, kind of weird), it turns out that we are at once too attached *and* too critical of our own work to know exactly how to improve it. We can't see the forest for the trees (or even notice clichés like "the forest for the trees" that should be omitted and/or rewritten).

But it can be challenging to find a method of peer response that works in the classroom, because students often do not know exactly what to look for. Especially in the early years of high school, their knowledge of spelling, grammar, and punctuation is often flawed, their understanding of the rhythm and music of language primitive at best, and their interest and investment in making someone else's paper better virtually nonexistent. Often, the comments they do provide are not only unhelpful but are, in fact, often simply wrong or even damaging.

As a writer myself, I am not immune to the problems of completing a peer response. Once, a friend of mine told me she decided she wanted to be a writer. In my earnest interest in helping her, I offered to mark up her work. She handed over a perfectly serviceable short story that I marked the bejesus out of, presumably under the auspices of "helping her improve." It wasn't until years later that I realized I had gone too far when she confessed that my "help" had only discouraged her, and she spent an unfortunate amount of time after that simply not writing. The good news is that now, decades later, she is still writing. Around the same time, another friend of mine, a skilled writer in her own right, said I had given her novel "the English teacher treatment" because again, in a genuine attempt to help a writer improve, I did a line edit that ended up redesigning her novel as *I* would have written it, rather than coaxing out what was best from what was already on the page.

Still, having another pair of eyes on your paper before you move into the revision stage is invaluable because you need someone who hasn't been living and breathing the work for the past several weeks, months, or even years. Thankfully, I finally figured out the balance, thanks to another writer friend. Lara Zielin is the author of several young adult books including *Donut Days*, *The Implosion of Aggie Winchester*, and *The Waiting Sky*. Furthermore, she is the creator of the Author Your Life journaling system that I mentioned earlier. Even though she lives in Michigan, and I live in Southern California, we were able to get into a perfect rhythm of peer response thanks to modern technology and the magic of snail mail. When we were both working on our first young adult novels, we mailed the manuscripts to each other, marked them up, and then sent them back. By then, thanks to several years as a classroom teacher and marking up thousands of essays, I had learned how to give Lara exactly the kind of feedback she needed without discouraging her, and Lara also knew how to make suggestions on my work with grace and care. She was also able to identify where my work required tough love and shared that with me as well.

One of the greatest compliments I have ever received was from my own father, who once asked me to edit a piece of writing he had to submit for a side job he was trying to snag after his official retirement. I was especially nervous critiquing my father's paper not only because I have great respect for him but because I knew that his formal education ended after high school, and he probably hadn't written anything longer than a grocery list for decades.

After marking up his paper, sending it back, and holding my breath, he called to thank me and then, as an aside, he said, "And the best part is that you made the writing better, but it still sounds like me."

I decided that his assessment would be my peer response goal forever after: make the writing better while still making it sound like the writer.

In the classroom, if the peer response model doesn't live up to your expectations, consider moving to a form of self-evaluation. Here's how it works: I ask my students a series of questions that require them to interact with their own paper in a meaningful way. It's a method for them to be mindful about their own writing. Most of them would probably rather not even look at their writing again after completing that very first draft. So I say things like "Put a box around your MLA in-text citation," "Underline the opinion in your topic sentence twice," and "Put a check mark in the margin next to your major thesis." A self-evaluation is not terribly sexy or exciting—in fact, it's rather tedious, but it really helps them improve what needs to be improved.

For those classes where I feel can go deeper, I use more advanced strategies. I might say things like "Cut your weakest sentence of commentary and write another, better sentence," "Rewrite your hook to be more engaging," or "I guarantee you can cut at least five words that just don't need to be in the paper. Look for them now and cross them out."

My self-evaluation activity takes about thirty minutes. It doesn't require DVD players, Flipgrid, Google Classroom, Schoology, or

Chromebooks. It's just the individual grappling with the words he or she has put on the page and looking for ways to make them better.

It's almost like a scavenger hunt that takes place within their essay.

And the reward at the end of the hunt is almost always a better piece of writing.

CHAPTER 21

Revision

Crime novelist Elmore Leonard must have been a great fan of revision, considering that he once said, "If it sounds like writing, I rewrite it."

This gets to the heart of revision. By the time you've polished your piece of writing to a high sheen, which is really the final step in a robust revision process, it shouldn't sound like writing at all. It should sound more like an intimate conversation with your reader. Conversely, if you're showing off all the effort you put into the piece by being fancy or unclear or using giant words, you've taken a wrong turn. In true mindful fashion, by the end of your process, you should let your writing just be what it is.

Think of all great art. Whether it's a painting, a song, a poem, a sculpture, a film or stage performance, or a ballet, if it's truly a great work of art, it appears effortless. While I am personally fascinated with an artist's process, most of the audience is not interested in the struggle the artist went through to get there. They do not want to see the hours of training and practice, the weeks of play rehearsal, the several ceramic pots you smashed on the studio floor in frustration and disgust, the sore and calloused feet inside your soiled and beat-up toe shoes. They are simply interested in the magic of the final product, which is so beautiful and artful that they just watch in awe, wondering (sometimes aloud) "How did she do that?"

If it's done well, our writing should seem similarly effortless.

In *Bird by Bird*, Anne Lamott talks about the benefits of what she calls "shitty first drafts." Her point is that no first draft is good enough to see the light of day and that we should give ourselves grace if it doesn't come out perfectly the first time. She believes in the glorious benefits of revision, refinement, and the wisdom of what a friend of hers calls the "up draft" and the "down draft." The down draft, she says, is when you get it all down, and the up draft is when you fix it all up. The third draft, Lamott tells us, is the "dental draft," where you check each tooth.

Most of my students would be happy if they just cranked something out, turned it in, sat back, laced their fingers behind their heads, and sighed, "I'm done," and then never saw that piece of writing again.

But you must, of course, revise. And while there are many editing and revision methods available, two specific types always come to mind for me.

These two types of editing do different things; they solve different problems. Therefore, you should, of course, use both of them.

Global Editing

Global editing (sometimes known as "developmental" or "substantive" editing) is when you take a big-picture view of the entire piece. You're looking at the piece as a whole organism. Is it strong? Does it hold together? How good is the skeleton of the piece? Does it have "good bones"? It's kind of an all-or-nothing pass (or series of passes). Does it have a strong hook that grabs the reader's attention? Is the conclusion powerful, profound, and as striking as the last few notes of an impactful piece of music?

During global editing, you are looking at elements like:

- overall structure
- beginnings, middles, and ends (of the entire thing, but also of chapters, paragraphs, and even sentences)
- how the writing looks on the page
- presentation factors like titles, formatting, font size, and style
- the hook and the conclusion.

If you're writing fiction, maybe there is a plot point problem right in the middle of the story, or maybe your character is flat and one-dimensional, and you spend some time fleshing out more details that bring your character—and by extension, your story—to life. Maybe the setting needs to be punched up. Maybe you need to create a more compelling beginning that gets your reader to turn the page.

If you're writing nonfiction, some of the same considerations apply. You will still need to intrigue your reader by creating a beginning that lures the reader in and gives them questions they want answered. Common nonfiction hooks include startling information, questions, anecdotes, or powerful examples. It's worth reiterating here that humans are hardwired for stories, and so telling stories both in the beginning of your piece and throughout is a profound way to keep your readers glued to your writing.

Line Editing

After you have made sweeping changes during global editing, it's time to get down to the nitty-gritty work of going sentence by sentence and word by word. During line editing, you will be looking at how you can improve each line, each sentence, each word, and the overall impact of the language. For the record, line editing is one of my favorite parts of the writing process.

Line editing considers elements like:

- the rhythm and music of the language in each sentence
- the "build" of sentences that ultimately lead to some kind of satisfying payoff
- how the sentences fit together as bricks in the entire wall
- diction (individual word choice)
- the connotation of individual words
- tone.

One reason I enjoy revision so much is because I love tinkering with words. I love language. I love checking on each word and making sure it's doing what it's supposed to be doing. I love working with a word, a phrase, a sentence, a paragraph, a chapter, sometimes an entire book until it sings. I love working with a piece until I've fixed everything I can. Basically, I just love communicating.

Another reason that revision is my favorite part of the writing process is because of the word itself: *revision*. Let's break it down: the word is composed of two parts, the word *vision* and the prefix *re-*. So really, when you engage in revision, you are seeing your writing again. You are looking at it a second time (or third or fourth) to ensure that it is as concise, communicative, and artful as you can possibly make it.

I often think of Beat poet Allen Ginsberg's well-known proclamation of "first thought, best thought." Ginsberg was not espousing anti-revision rhetoric, so what was his point? I think he was saying that it's okay to be spontaneous, to be in the moment, and to rely on your intuition. Ginsberg was saying that you should, by all means, get the thought down in the heat of composition, don't do any immediate editing, and connect to the passion, emotion, and fire that each new idea brings.

Once you get skilled at "seeing it again," though, and you polish the words and sentences to a shine, you can turn an ordinary piece of writing into a work of art.

CHAPTER 22

Precision

When you're a heart surgeon, you can't approximate. You can't cut in the *almost* right place. You have no choice but to have a steady hand and be precise with your work. Same if you're an engineer. Design a bridge or a spaceship with specifications that are close but not exact, and the spaceship crashes and the bridge collapses. In those cases, it's easy to tell when you weren't precise enough because it's often a matter of life and death.

Precision in writing is also critical. As in most communication, it is important that we practice saying *exactly* what we mean. There is no room for mush-mouthed beating around the bush when thoughts, relationships, and sometimes even lives hang in the balance. Even if our only goal is to get a higher grade on our *To Kill A Mockingbird* essay, we must learn not to approximate our thoughts, but to take the time and make the effort to find the words to express exactly what's in our heart and minds. We must say *exactly* what we mean.

According to the online edition of the Oxford English Dictionary, the origin of the word *precision* comes from the French *précision* or Latin *praecisio(n-)*, from *praecidere*, "cut off."

How does precision apply to student writing, especially when we're approaching writing through the lens of mindfulness? First, we start by having a vision. Then we need to ask questions: What are we trying to accomplish? What does the end product look like? Where are we headed? Once we have the answers to some of those questions, it's time to work on precision. As the etymology of the word *precision* suggests, the next step is to cut. We need to take out what we don't need and remove anything that isn't serving the overall message. We must excise the extraneous, the opaque, the vague, the blurry, and the fuzzy. We must be accurate, precise, and exacting in the written expression of our ideas. In fact, in the interest of precision, I probably should have cut those last two sentences.

Think of it, again, like an expert who works with bonsai trees. She starts with a vision of what she wants the tree to look like. And then, through careful and exact trimming, pruning, and cutting, as well as wiring the tree to grow in certain ways, she shapes the bonsai tree as closely as she can to that initial vision she had in her mind. Like good writing, it's a slow, methodical, intentional process, but it is informed by a great deal of spirit, emotion, and intuition.

Here's another metaphor for the more practical among you. Most manufacturing companies have a person whose sole job it is to do quality control. These folks make sure that every single widget that goes out the door meets certain predetermined specifications; they ensure that all the parts are doing what they're supposed to be doing and that they're uniform. In the world of writing, that job falls to the editor or, in the case of you and your students, you as the teacher. But think about how much we can help a piece of writing improve if we put more of the onus for precision back on the writer?

What if we expect that, before a piece of writing even gets to us, the writer has made every attempt to be precise?

How good would the writing be then?

What if your students set a revision goal to say exactly what they meant, and not just an approximation, a guess, a "close enough"? Forget the grade. What if they composed sentences that were so finely sculpted that they were able to make the reader think what they wanted them to think, feel what they wanted them to feel, or do what they wanted them to do?

The more clarity we have in our thoughts, the clearer we can be in the expression of those thoughts through the colorful, complex, and captivating—but ultimately imperfect—vehicle of the English language. As Mark Twain once famously said, "The difference between the *almost right* word and the *right* word is really a large matter. 'Tis the difference between the lightning bug and the lightning."

So what exactly does precision look like?

- Start by asking, "What am I trying to say?" and then find the answer.
- Choose the right word (to be clear: the *right* word, not the *biggest* word).
- Tighten up the sentences so there's no flab or extraneous words.
- Choose the best form for the piece (in other words, a haiku should not be a screenplay and vice versa).
- Set a goal of relentless and clear-eyed revision.
- Find the best—not perfect—rhythm for the music of the paragraphs.
- Choose a title that gives insight into the piece.

If you are muddy or vague or confusing or opaque in your communication, a talk with your children may be unsuccessful, your business negotiations may fail, your marriage proposal may be misunderstood.

Imagine living the rest of your life alone because the language you used did not precisely express your thoughts.

Okay, perhaps I'm exaggerating.

But what if I'm not?

I always tell my students that the reason I am teaching them to be effective communicators is not to please their parents or get a good grade or get into a good college. Not even close. The reason I am teaching them to be effective communicators is because, in this world, it is the effective communicators who often get what they want.

And because I care about them, I want them to get what they want.

CHAPTER 23

Clarity

Here's something for you to ponder: Do we write to gain clarity about our thoughts, or does clarity help make our writing better?

Since writing is primarily about communication, clarity is critical. And to achieve maximum clarity, you must consider other aspects of the piece, such as purpose, audience, and methods. Let's look at these more closely.

Purpose. Purpose refers to the reason you're writing the piece. Of course, for your students, the answer might as simple as "Because my teacher told me to." But taking a broader approach, the purpose might be to inform, the entertain, to move, or to persuade. You can increase your level of clarity by knowing exactly why you're writing what you're writing.

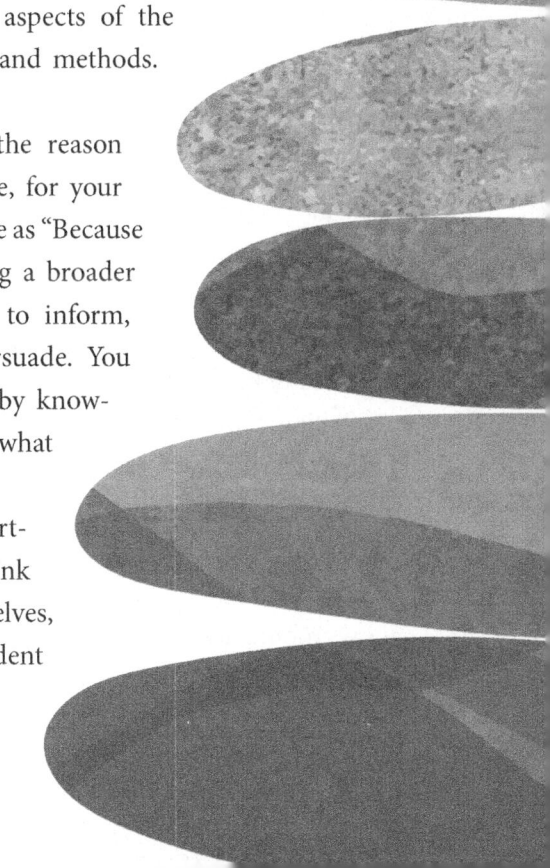

Audience. Despite how important this aspect is, I don't really think many beginning writers ask themselves, "Who is this for?" Again, student writers may think, "This is only for my teacher," and they may be right. But in addition to completing assignments, your students should write for authentic audiences. This may take the form of a published blog, a social media post, or any other piece of writing that may be viewed by the world at large. When teaching my ninth graders the business letter format, for example, I often had them write the letter to a real person or business and provide me with a business envelope and the proper postage, and then I would send it, giving extra credit to anybody who received a response by the end of the school year. I told them that the extra credit was because if they got a response that probably meant the writing was effective and the letter was successful in its mission to move its audience to action.

Form and methods. Before any writer puts pen to paper or fingers to keyboard, he or she must decide on the form that will be employed. Will it be a novel? A poem? An argumentative essay? An infographic? An advertisement? Will your dominant rhetorical appeal be ethos, pathos, or logos? What kind of evidence or support will be used? Will the work rely on humor or be more heartrending? Each of these critical decisions will inevitably shape and inform the piece, and so, in the interest of clarity, it is important that the writer knows exactly what form and methods will work best for the intended piece.

If you believe in your message enough to keep trying to communicate it, and if you take the time and care to present it with the utmost intention and effort, you may ultimately reach and connect with your reader. And that's the bliss of writing.

Telling a writer to be clearer and more precise is almost always good feedback. I've never seen a situation where a writer was *too* clear. And clarity is often a matter of detail and imagery—not fruit, but apple. Not apple, but Golden Delicious. Not Golden Delicious, but Golden Delicious with a wormhole and a slight bruise by the stem. There's not always room for every single detail or image, so the surgical skill comes in knowing what to include and what to leave out.

In our writing, if we find the detail that nails the idea we're trying to communicate (and, by default, eliminate all of the extraneous details), then we've reached new levels of precision and clarity.

Clarity is being able to direct the reader's focus.

What do you want them to see? Where do you want them to look?

I recently went to Disneyland, and I noticed something about clarity. When you're on a ride—especially the so-called "dark" rides that you might find in Fantasyland or, say, the Pirates of the Caribbean—your little car or boat is on a track, and as you travel through the ride, the track aims you, almost cinematically, toward exactly what the Disney Imagineers want you to see. You are pointed, as it were, toward the key elements of the story that is unfolding in front of you. When it's time to see something else, the track turns, and you find yourself looking at another specific element of the story—whether it's Pinocchio in a cage on Pleasure Island, the dynamite-munching goat on Big Thunder Mountain Railroad, or the grim, grinning ghosts of the Haunted Mansion.

What if we directed our readers the same way and gave them an exact idea of what we want them to see (and, by extension, think about)? Telling a clear story is a form of mindfulness, and we can use that as an object lesson on clarity in our writing. How can you best direct the reader's focus so that the reader not only grasps, but is moved by, your point?

You have to keep asking, "What do I want the reader to see?" If you don't, the writing will become blurry, vague, opaque, and foggy. And that's not what you're after. You want the reader to be crystal clear on your message and know exactly what you're trying to say.

When you are clear in your sentence structure, word choice, and the relationship between ideas, the reader can envision what you're talking about and can see what you mean, and then they are more likely to be persuaded by your points or moved by your story.

But first you must have a clear sense of what you're trying to say.

Isn't it wonderful when we've been struggling with an idea, and suddenly, as if by a magical switch, our mind's light flips on, and we are almost at once able to see exactly how to move forward? The answer seems so obvious! The idea so crystal clear! Getting clarity has many benefits: it increases our knowledge and wisdom, eases our frustration, and gives us direction. Clarity is a wonderful thing to achieve not only in our writing but, by extension, our lives.

Danny's Writing Diary:

Slave2theMuse

I first heard the word blogging in 2005. "Do you mean to tell me," I thought, "that after a lifetime of being a writer and hoping for an audience, I can just start publishing what I have to say on the internet? For free?"

Unbelievable.

I created a Blogspot account and thought of a name for my new publishing platform. Did a part of me think that things would take off—this was quite a while before social media—and the blog would make me famous?

Maybe a little.

That's not exactly how things shook out, but there was an interesting function where you could discover other blogs by random people all over the world, and I found several writers whose blogs were interesting, well-written, entertaining, amusing, profane, and even horrifying. I followed them and often enjoyed their ramblings, musings, and reflections.

Slave2theMuse, my very first blog (I've probably had ten or twelve since), is still up on Blogspot. I started posting on July 3, 2005. My last post was on November 25, 2007. Those two years of writing practice were incalculably helpful. While not terribly PC these days, the name was a wry nod to the musician Prince (and his creative spelling in song titles like "Nothing Compares 2 U") and the idea that writing was an illness and a compulsion for me. I couldn't not do it. Therefore, in my mind, anyway, I was obligated to listen to that impulse deep inside to write. As a result, the moniker "Slave2theMuse" summed up my writing habits nicely.

Most of my posts concerned my writing practice, including the mystery novel I was sending to agents and the young adult novel I was working on at the time. I tended to sneak in posts after school, on my lunch breaks, in the evenings, and on weekends. The blog was read almost exclusively by my father and my teacher friend who taught in the next classroom. I was always grateful for the support they both gave me.

Some of the more interesting posts included:

> **7/03/05:** A version of the story you'll read in this book about when my first poem was accepted for publication in a literary magazine called Proof Rock.
>
> **3/22/06:** A post called "Status Report" consisting of an update about my submissions of flash fiction, poetry, and short stories to various literary journals and competitions.
>
> **5/10/06:** The news that my first piece of flash fiction, called "Lockdown," had been published in the now defunct journal rumble (lowercase r, of course, because the editor was, no doubt, trying to be edgy and artsy).
>
> **7/24/07:** An entry about submitting my novel to big-time New York agents and how I hadn't heard back in a very long time from any of them. The post was called—what else?—"No Muse is Good Muse."

But the most interesting thing about my first blog is that more people were reading it than I thought. I was surprised one day to see a comment on one of my posts by someone I didn't know. I had an audience! A small audience, but still.

That person, author and entrepreneur Lara Zielin, mentioned that we seemed to be on a similar path with our writing, and would I like to compare notes sometime? Writing can be a very lonely and isolating business, so of course I said yes. As I mention elsewhere, before long, we were sharing manuscripts and giving each other feedback. Lara eventually went on to publish a number of young adult books and several romance novels, and is now the creator and CEO of the Author Your Life journaling platform. We have never met in person, but through the magic of social media, email, and a number of Skype (and later Zoom) calls, we have been friends for over seventeen years.

One of the most meaningful things I learned from Slave2theMuse and the miracle of blogging was the power and gift of getting that first reader.

CHAPTER 24

Words to Avoid

In Eastern philosophy, the concept of yin and yang suggests that in life there are opposites, and those opposites create balance within the whole. If you've seen the symbol, and I'm sure you have, you've probably noticed that in the yin side there's a smidgen of yang, and vice versa. That's also about balance. For my money, yin and yang is one of the most important philosophies out there.

Just as it is in Eastern philosophy, yin and yang is an important idea in writing, particularly when it comes to what *not* to do. In other words, while there are always lessons about what to include to make quality writing and approaches that you *should* do (yin), a plethora of actions also exist that you should not do (yang), including a list of words you should not use in formal expository writing—if you want your writing to sing, that is. And of course, within each, there is a little bit of the other. Hence, the yin and yang of writing.

The following is a list of common words and writing habits that writers should avoid for clean, clear, and effective communication. I'm sure you'll be familiar with many of them, but I'm hoping this list will be a nice reminder for your students' work and your own. These suggestions apply mostly to academic, expository-style essays. Always consider genre, audience, and purpose. If you write fiction, poetry, or song lyrics, for example, all bets are off where this chapter is concerned. Know your audience, and then use what works.

"Thing" words. Thing, anything, nothing, something, everything. Like placeholders in math, these empty words are stand-ins for what you really mean. My former mother-in-law did this all the time. She would always say, "Danny, can you hand me that thing over there?" And I would look toward where she was pointing and think, "What? What do you want? The magazine? The remote control? The pillow? The ceramic monkey?" (Yes, there was a ceramic monkey lounging on an end table near her La-Z-Boy. I'm still not sure why.) The point is, I had no idea what she wanted. Thing words are just you, as the writer saying, "You know what I mean. So I'm not actually going to say it," But in actuality, we don't know what you mean. It's your job, as the writer, to explain it to us, clearly and precisely. If you replace "thing" words with what you really mean, you increase your chances of effectively communicating with your reader and getting exactly what you want.

Good, bad, happy, sad. Good how? Bad how? Exactly how are you happy? Are you elated? Thrilled? Joyful? Excited? Content? Again, precision makes all the difference.

Clichés. Clichés are expressions that have been used so often they have lost their freshness, vitality, and originality. Let's take when a student is writing about George and Lennie in Steinbeck's *Of Mice and Men* and says, "George was there for Lennie through thick and thin." Not only has this expression been used so much that it falls flat, but it's just plain vague. George was there how? What did George do exactly? Using clichés is lazy writing because it typically means the writer did not care enough to make the effort to express an idea in his or her own way, using his or her own metaphorical vision, for example, or a unique sense of observation or detail. The irony, of course, that I discovered after teaching only a few years is that it's very difficult for young writers to identify clichés in their own writing (or other writing, for that matter) because you need to have a certain amount of life experience to know that certain expressions are overused. That takes time. The bottom line is that most clichés are as old as the hills. That's all I'm saying.

Slang. You know that *sick, phat, dope, fresh, tight, fly*, and whatever else today's teenagers are saying is slang. Of course by the time you are holding this book in your hands, even those expressions will probably be passé. In my day, of course, everything was *far out, out of sight*, and *radical*. We know slang does not belong in formal expository writing. But what about what we might call "informal language"? It's an issue of context. Your students probably aren't going to go to the cafeteria and tell their friends, after a less than satisfying lunch, that "getting that cheeseburger was really an error in judgment." Their friends would mock them unmercifully. A student would instead say, "Wow, I really messed up." But if that same student says, in an essay, "Gatsby really messed up by obsessing about Daisy," I'm going to mark *messed up* as informal language and inappropriate for a formal expository essay. (Note: I just write "slang" in the margin. It takes far fewer pen strokes than writing "informal language," and when you're marking hundreds of essays, every pen stroke counts.)

Very. Kill it. You almost never need this word. Instead of saying, "I'm very tired," say "I'm exhausted." It's that simple. As Mark Twain once famously said, "Substitute 'damn' every time you're inclined to write 'very'; your editor will delete it and the writing will be just as it should be."

Different. Consider this sentence: "The president had a very different approach to unemployment than her predecessor." Does the word *different* tell us anything? I hope you said no. You need to say what you mean by *different*. As we've seen with the other no-no's, it's a matter of being specific, clear, and detailed. What if it said this: "The president attacked unemployment by creating job programs, training the unskilled, and rewarding employers for creating more opportunities, all of which her predecessor failed to do." I hope you see the strength of the revision.

This is far from an exhaustive list of don'ts, but you get the idea.

One profound way for a writer to achieve a greater sense of mindfulness and Zen is to understand the concept of subtraction, which refers to the process of taking out what you don't need and leaving only the essence, the key idea, so that it is sharp and clear. It's similar to Hemingway's idea that what the reader is seeing is just the tip of the iceberg and that there's so much more below the surface of the sea.

The yin and yang of it all is that while many writing methods books show you what you should include, it is at least as important to think about what to leave out to achieve the right balance, and balance requires some flexibility. For example, sometimes it may be necessary to include a no-no word or phrase. Sometimes using a "thing" word may be appropriate (or unavoidable), or you might find that throwing in a bit of informal language helps you establish the proper tone or voice.

Are there any absolutes in this department?

I suppose.

But ultimately, the writer is the arbiter of what's best for any given piece, and that depends on what the writer is trying to accomplish and who the piece is for. It also requires the writer to be present in the moment, know the requirements of that specific piece, and to be intentional about implementing what is needed.

But avoiding even these few no-no words never fails to improve student writing.

And my own.

CHAPTER 25

Set It Aside

How many times have you been in a heated discussion with a friend or loved one and then, hours later, wished you'd had some time to think about what to say before spouting off? Have you said things you wish you hadn't? Do you wish you'd had a chance to reflect before offering your two cents?

Of course. We all have.

And while we may not always have the opportunity to do that in a heated discussion, we can always do it with our writing.

Let me explain.

You've done the writing.

You've decided the piece is as good as it's going to get.

You've celebrated the victory of being done with it.

So what do you do after you're done?

Easy.

You set it aside.

You let it cool off.

You let your words breathe.

You give your manuscript some time.

You let the dust settle around your writing, clear your mind, and get some distance and perspective on what you're trying to say.

When you set aside your writing, you allow it to mellow and age in a way that lets you detach from what you thought you wrote so you can go back and see what you actually wrote. And that's the critical part. You can't edit what you *thought* was there. You can only revise the words that *actually* exist.

It's a little like putting a cherry pie on the windowsill to cool.

Great. Now I want cherry pie.

But I digress.

How long you put the manuscript aside depends on your schedule. Some writing gurus suggest you put it aside for six weeks to let the words cool. But in the sentiments of internet sensation Sweet Brown, "Ain't nobody got time for that."

Especially if you're giving an assignment in class. I'm sure you know some of your students will wait until the last moment to complete their work. So how long can they put their essays or stories aside to give them time to "cool"? I recommend at least twenty-four hours. Even a single day will give them an opportunity to gain some perspective.

Perspective is critical in properly assessing your writing. But don't take my word for it. As Malcolm Gladwell says in his online MasterClass on writing, when it comes to reviewing your writing, "Perspective is your friend. And the only way to gain perspective is time."

Put your writing in a drawer, a file cabinet, a shoebox in the back of the closet.

Let your words, thoughts, and language incubate.

And then, when you take it back out, have that red pen ready and get back to work.

Peer Response Assignments

Should you find peer responses effective, here are some recommended steps:

1. Have your students trade papers, then tell them that the first requirement for peer response is to read the paper. Explain that first they simply need to familiarize themselves with what's on the page.

2. Next, give them space and time to read the piece out loud. Maybe everyone puts on earbuds so they aren't distracted. Maybe you take them outside, and they each find their own space to read out loud.

3. Next, have them mark parts that are "bumpy." If a section doesn't read smoothly, there's a problem. Tell them they don't need to say *why* it's bumpy. They just need to mark that it isn't working. Typically, the problem is precision, clarity, or both.

4. Have them mark what they perceive as the weakest sentence in each paragraph. Later, the writer will rewrite these sentences.

5. Have them cut 3–5 words on each page that simply do not need to be there. This will make sentences leaner and more muscular.

6. Have them interact with the text via annotation while they are looking for the things you want to make sure are there. (Ask them to box the in-text citations for material from other sources, underline thesis sentences, put a check in the margin next to each quotation, circle strong vocabulary, etc.)

7. Have them ask two questions that might improve the paper. Make sure that the questions are valid and helpful. "Why does your intro paragraph suck so hard?" is not helpful! However,

"Can you go more in-depth on your analysis of Romeo's impulsiveness?" is.

8. Have them write three positive comments. "Great sentence structure!" or "Excellent hook!" are good examples.

Revision Assignments

1. After your students have traded papers, have them seek and destroy the no-no words.

2. Whether in their own paper or a partner's, have your students look at the beginning and end of every paragraph, making sure each paragraph absolutely shines (especially in terms of precision and clarity). Then have them do the same thing for the beginning and end of the entire piece.

3. Ask them to reflect on these questions: Is this piece better now that I've spent some time in peer response and revision? Why? Is the vocabulary better? Is the overall structure clearer? Was I clearer and more precise in my analysis?

Finishing

CHAPTER 26

Being Done

In his book *David and Goliath: Underdogs, Misfits, and the Art of Battling Giants*, author Malcom Gladwell talks about a phenomenon called "the inverted U-curve." Typically, this means that to a certain degree an approach may be good, beneficial, and helpful, but that at some point, it loses its effectiveness and can actually cause damage.

I believe the inverted U-curve is especially true when it comes to writing.

It's good to rewrite and revise your writing with a goal of improving it. In fact, there are a multitude of reasons to revise. You may work toward making your piece clearer, more precise, more fluid, more engaging, and even more powerful. But sometimes I've seen, even in my own work, a piece of writing ruined by overediting. Constantly reworking the overall structure, putting in and then taking out and then putting back in commas, or simply gutting a piece in the interest of perfectionism can do more harm than good.

At some point you just have to be done and send the piece on its way.

That doesn't mean that it's perfect. Far from it.

The sad fact is that you may not even be happy with it.

In other words, the pursuit is not to create a perfect piece of writing.

The pursuit is, and always should be, an ever-evolving and constantly improving writing practice.

When I work with my students on an essay, a short story, a research paper, or any other piece of writing, sometimes I find myself leaning over and, as gently and mindfully as possible, half-whispering to a young writer, "We should probably move on. That's as good as this one's going to get."

I've sometimes had to whisper it to myself as well, knowing in my heart that there will always be other work in the future that can be even better.

CHAPTER 27

Celebrate the Victories

There's a scene in the movie based on Stephen King novel *Misery* where writer Paul Sheldon finishes the first draft of his new novel and, after typing "The End," celebrates the completion of the manuscript by popping open a bottle of champagne and taking a sip to toast his new book.

Why?

Because everyone loves to celebrate.

More importantly, everyone loves to *be* celebrated.

We don't give a second thought to celebrating birthdays, anniversaries, holidays, and sports team victories. Celebrating those events and milestones are rituals of our culture. There are gifts, music, drinks, and usually good food involved. But there are so many other things we can celebrate, if only we are intentional.

When it comes to writing, celebrating the wins is a key part of the process, one that I highly recommend you incorporate into your practice.

Let me tell you this: whether it gets published or not, completing a full-length book manuscript is a massive achievement all by itself, and anyone who completes it, as Paul Sheldon shows, deserves a pat on the back. Even if they are doing the patting themselves.

And while things didn't turn out so hot for *Misery*'s Mr. Sheldon, it was important to him to take a moment and acknowledge the successful completion of a step in the process. In King's fictional universe, the author had written and published many books in the past, including other installments in the Misery series, but he knew the importance of celebrating the victories in the current moment. It was important to celebrate *this* book, *this* win, at *this* time. I don't know for certain, but I'm guessing that we are privy to that scene because Stephen King sometimes feels the same way, and I'm willing to bet that Mr. King has his own celebratory rituals during his own wildly successful process.

But should celebrations be limited to best-selling novelists?

Of course not.

There's no reason at all that each and every one of us can't find moments along the way to give a giant "Hell yeah!" whoop to the universe when we have a writing win.

From 1998 to 2001, for example, I spent three years writing the first draft of my novel *Bad Moon Rising*. At the time, the vision was to write a series of mystery novels using the titles of classic rock songs. Like many aspiring novelists, I wrote when I could—before and after work, after our infant daughter went to bed, on winter and spring breaks, even during the summer. After working on the book and living with those characters for three years, I can vouch for the fact that typing "The End" was an emotional and cathartic experience.

It deserved commemoration.

Since I finished the novel during the school year, I decided to include my English department colleagues (many of whom knew of and supported my writing aspirations) in my celebration. One of my fellow English teachers who loved reading agreed to read my novel as I wrote it and very kindly kept asking for the next installment. Talk about motivation! I have a specific memory of being so excited to be done with the book that I printed out the last few pages and rushed them down to her classroom.

Later that week, we all agreed that we would meet one night after work at a local restaurant during happy hour to celebrate.

But keep in mind:

We weren't celebrating that the book was being made into a movie.

We weren't celebrating that the book was a best seller.

We weren't even celebrating that the book had been published.

We were simply celebrating the fact that the book was *done*.

The manuscript had been completed.

That was enough.

It was wonderful to have my friends there for the celebration. At least that's what they tell me. The details of the celebration are a little fuzzy. I am in no way a drinker, and that evening a few of my friends sent me shots of Jägermeister, a beverage I'd never heard of before and, with any luck, will never encounter again.

Years later, when my first book, *The Zen Teacher*, was published, I knew I wanted to celebrate. But this time, I actually waited until I received my first royalty check. It was the end of 2015, and I'd had my eye on this newfangled gadget called an Amazon Echo. Apparently, you could talk to it, and it would just do stuff, and that sounded pretty dang cool to me. So a small chunk of my first royalty check went to buying this odd-looking black tower that was part speaker, part AI and, quite possibly, part government surveillance system. That Echo is, some years later, still sitting on my counter at home and still answers to the name of Alexa.

I remember the time, years earlier, I was in my friend Judy's apartment and saw a bound manuscript on her kitchen table.

I knew she was a writer, and I almost couldn't believe my eyes.

"What's that?"

"That's my book." Judy's voice carried almost as much disbelief as I was feeling. "I finally finished it."

I'd seen published books my entire life, but that was the first time I had ever seen a completed book-length manuscript in the wild. I was in awe. The sky almost opened, and I'm pretty sure that somewhere over the dingy Burbank sky, a handful of chubby cherubs sang. I still have a mental picture of that stack of papers, held together along the spine with three brass brads, sitting on Judy's kitchen table.

Even then, I knew that the radical act of actually *completing* a book-length manuscript was a massive achievement and should be acknowledged.

If your students finish a big writing assignment—an essay or story or poem—find some way to celebrate the achievement. The celebration will leave your students with a pleasant memory of accomplishment and will encourage them to do it again. I am reminded of a story I heard, which, if it isn't true, should be, that sometimes teachers of the Torah give their students a morsel of chocolate when teaching so that their young charges associate the Torah with the taste of something sweet.

I always tell my students that they should be amazed at their ability to write something, especially when it comes to creative writing, because whatever it is—that story, that poem, that song lyric—is a piece of art that only days ago did not exist in the world and *they* made it.

And that's pretty badass.

CHAPTER 28

Detachment

In her book *Wild Mind: Living the Writer's Life*, author Natalie Goldberg writes, "We are not our writing. Our writing is a moment moving through us."

These are difficult words to internalize and believe in the deepest parts of ourselves.

Especially for our students, for whom there is almost always a grade at stake.

The reason is because in our culture we've conditioned our students to believe that grades measure who they are and what they're worth. It's also true that when our words, and by extension the pieces we compose, are so close to our hearts, and the ideas we are expressing are bubbling up from the deepest parts of our emotions, souls, and psyches, the idea that our writing isn't, in fact, *us* is overwhelming.

This happened to me when my first "real" book was published. I had written several books before, and I had even self-published one or two. But when *The Zen Teacher* hit the shelves (or, perhaps more accurately, Amazon), it just hit different. This book encapsulated so much of what I thought about teaching, teachers, writing, and even living as a grounded, relaxed person. It was almost a spiritual experience.

But confusing our writing with ourselves or our self-worth is not only a mistake, it's dangerous. They are two separate entities. *The Zen Teacher* is a part of me, sure, but it's not *me*. If I thought it was, my self-esteem would take a massive hit every time someone said something negative about the book, every time I didn't sell any copies at a conference, and any time the Amazon numbers took a dip. Who wants that kind of roller-coaster experience with such a vulnerable part of your identity? Not me.

So what's the antidote?

Detachment.

Detachment means that you do not allow your ego to dictate what you will and won't be happy with. Put another way, the Buddhist concept of "nonattachment" refers to not clinging to thoughts or expectations about how something will go. But it's also a little more complicated than Elsa from *Frozen*'s directive to just "Let it go."

Detachment is not, as Westerners sometimes misconstrue it, about being afraid to care about things or about not committing. Quite the opposite. It's about being okay with things being exactly as they are and knowing that what *is*, is exactly what is supposed to be happening. And by approaching life with this sense of nonattachment, you will probably end up being happier. But not everyone can grasp this subtle and abstract hairsplitting. In fact, I remember once reading about a young woman who was engaged to a fiancé who didn't quite grasp this concept. He said, "But we're getting married. I *want* to be attached to you."

Listen here, fiancé boy, you're totally not getting it. Detachment is not about being distant or aloof or uncaring. Rather, it's about not white-knuckling your assumptions about how life should go, how your relationship should be, or what outcomes you seek.

In the Zen Teacher workshops, I always share the following quote: "Most of the suffering in the world is the result of thwarted expectations." That was a mic drop moment for me because of its fundamental accuracy. I'm not saying that if someone in the world is hungry that their suffering is the result of their expectation that there should always be food available.

That's a whole other thing.

Look at it this way: I was once going through a rather difficult time in my life. I wanted something that would help me forget my troubles, lift my spirits, and, ultimately, make me happy. Having always been interested in music and having had a desire to play the guitar since I was a child, I thought it was time that I got back to that. So I saved my money and started haunting local pawn shops to find a suitable guitar.

"When I get a guitar," I thought, "*then* I will be happy." And while saving and searching for the guitar, and knowing I was close to getting it, was an entertaining distraction, the actual acquisition of the guitar, as you can imagine, changed nothing. I had attached an expectation of my happiness to an outside object that had nothing to do with what was going on inside of me. But I believed it would make me happy. And even though I enjoyed having the guitar, when I realized it really hadn't changed the fundamental emotional state I was experiencing, I was confused and disheartened.

Enter suffering.

Or, if not suffering, exactly, certainly disappointment. And to top it all off, I was now out eighty dollars for a guitar. I was married, had children, and was fully an adult in every way, and should have known better than to think that amassing stuff would make me any happier. As a wise person once said, "Happiness is an inside job."

How do I know that you are not your writing? Well, if you were, I would be much more freaked out about my friends who are writing fiction and whose themes are darker. I don't look at them side-eyed when I find out they've spent all afternoon researching serial killers or googling

"Ten Effective Ways to Poison Your Husband." I know it's part of the process and not about who the writer is as a functioning human being.

Another effective technique for writers is the practice of detaching from the expectations and judgment of others. While we work in a world where you, as a teacher, still need to assess and even put a letter grade on a piece of student writing, you can subtly remind your students that they are not just writing for the grade, but to become better thinkers and communicators. When it comes down to it, what do your students owe you with their writing? They owe it to you to make their best effort, I suppose, and to turn in the assignment. But other than that, not much. And guess what? If they are practicing being better thinkers and communicators through their written words, the grade takes care of itself. Magic. So not attaching to what other people think about our writing can almost, counterintuitively, take us exactly where you want to go.

So write.

Write every day, if you want.

Write from your heart.

Write until the cows come home.

(But in that case, make sure you have some Febreze handy because that can be smelly.)

But don't attach to any of it.

Most importantly, do not attach to any particular outcome. Do not attach to the number of books, essays, or poems you are or *are not* writing. Do not obsess over Amazon sales numbers or social media likes. Do not attach to whether your piece is published or not. Spoiler alert: publishing is fun and an immediate rush, but if you're unhappy, getting published will not make you *happier*.

The most important reason for you and your students to write is to figure out your own sense of rhythm, voice, style, and content. Teachers don't like to hear that, but here we are. You must have faith that, when a student approaches a piece of writing by tuning into his or her own intuition and sense of purpose and audience, eventually the quality of writing will improve. I've watched it happen myself for over thirty years.

Remember: you are not in competition with anyone. You don't have to write more or better than Nicholas Sparks or Jodi Picoult. Your student doesn't have to write more or better than Josh in the honors class or Tiffany in AP. Each writer only needs to be better than he or she was yesterday. That's it. That's the entire goal. This message is particularly important to impart to our pupils who may be looking over their shoulders and comparing their success and progress (or lack thereof) with a neighbor, peer, or sibling.

As a result, one other important aspect of detachment is detachment from the finished piece. It went how it went. No use crying over spilled—wait, that's a cliché. Delete. The point is: there will be more writing projects. If you teach writing or are a writer yourself, you will encounter many other opportunities to express what's inside you. Therefore, there is no reason to attach to each individual piece as if it defines you or your writing practice. Because it doesn't.

It's an inescapable truth that students write because it's required. At some point, they must—to pass the class or, ultimately, to graduate. But when it works best, it's fun and enjoyable.

So what if we taught them—and you taught yourself—to write because it's therapeutic, because it feels good, because it helps us figure out what we think and what we want to do?

What would life (and education) look like then?

What if we refused to attach to the common, stereotypical expectations of why we should write (publication, fame, good grades, etc.)? How would our students grow as writers? And as people? Given the current structure of the American education system, that may be a crazy expectation, but we will never reach that place if we don't at least think it's possible.

CHAPTER 29

Multiple Drafts

If my students had their way, essays would be one-and-done affairs. Nothing would make them happier than writing a draft of the paper, shutting off the Chromebook, and saying, "Peace out." And as a teenager, I felt the same way. I just wanted to be done with homework so I could go watch TV or go outside. My attitude regarding my writing was that it was "good enough."

And I *liked* writing!

Imagine how the students feel who don't.

It would be nice if that was all it took to make a good piece of writing: brain-dump your thoughts onto the paper, sigh, shut off the computer, and go hang out with your friends.

But that's not how good writing works.

Good writing takes effort.

It takes editing, pruning, polishing.

In short, it takes multiple drafts.

The second, third, fourth, and sometimes fifth drafts are, quite frankly, where the magic happens. It's where you sculpt a fair or mediocre piece of writing into something that says something—an ultimate product that, if you're lucky, people want to read.

I understand that this is where some of the paralysis comes in the writing process. Young writers often say, "If I can't make it good on the first draft, why even bother? I don't want to go through all that other hassle. I don't know how to make it better. What do I even do? How do I improve it? Where do I go from here?"

The first thing I would say is do not be afraid of multiple drafts. In fact, in my own writing, tinkering with a piece after the first draft is completed is usually my favorite part. In the same way a painter might like picking the right color or canvas size, I enjoy mulling over the right word.

But when a writer commits to multiple drafts, the writing just gets better.

It almost cannot help but be improved.

With each pass through your manuscript, you should be looking at one or two specific issues at a time. That's all your mind can process.

Here are some suggestions:

- **Overall structure and length.** When you take a bird's-eye view of your piece, how does it look? Is it too long? Too short? Is the text too dense? Do you need more white space? Is it pleasing to the eye? Taking a high-level look at your piece of writing is a great first step for figuring out what it needs.
- **Logical progression of ideas.** Read through the first paragraph. Does it make sense? Does it logically transition from one idea to the next? Do the points connect, or is it a hodgepodge of disparate information and details that seem to jump all over the place? Can you reorder any of the sentences to make the ideas clearer? Does the paragraph need to start with a unifying sentence (often called the topic sentence) to tell your reader what they're going to be reading?

- **Sentence structure.** Is there a dynamic rhythm to your sentences? Do you have variety in the types of sentences? Are the phrases and clauses showing direct (and implied) connections between the ideas? Does your syntax have a "music" to it?
- **Word choice.** It's worth repeating: Finding the right word is more important than using a big word. Are you using words that are powerful, exacting, precise, and clear? Are you using the most effective words? Do you use words that have strong ideas and connotations behind them? If not, keep revising.
- **Tone.** Is your tone (which is a function of word choice) intentional? Have you made the tone sarcastic, mournful, or joyous on purpose through the words you choose? Does the tone support or detract from you message? Does it underscore it or amplify it?
- **Formatting.** Have you made it easy and enjoyable for your reader to consume your piece? Is the manuscript presentable? Is the font clear? Are all the parts in the right place (page numbers, headings, subheads, etc.)? Most importantly, is your formatting consistent? For example, if you're using the British spelling of *colour*, have you done that throughout? If not, make it uniform.

These are only some ideas intended to get you moving.

I never do fewer than two drafts with my students. Never. They always take steps to make a piece better. (Quick writes, free writes, journal entries, etc., are exempted from this for obvious reasons. These are exercises used to generate ideas, and the writing they produce is meant for the individual writer's eyes only.) When we are finished, I often read their pieces out loud to them. I want them to get used to hearing their own words, so they can begin to identify what I refer to as "the bumpy parts," and reading a piece out loud is the best way to fix those. If you can't say it gracefully, chances are your reader won't be able to follow it.

When going over a piece that a student and I have revised together, I always ask a few reflective questions:

1. Do you think this version is better than what we started with? (The answer, of course, is always yes, which, oddly, surprises them.)
2. What is better about it? (I want them to mention things like fluidity, vocabulary, precision, clarity, and rhythm.)
3. How did we do it? I want them to realize we got there by messing around with sentence structure and adjusting how we expressed the relationships between ideas, by finding stronger words, by cutting filler, by adding imagery or detail or evidence.

I always say that writers have an extra step compared to most artists. For example, when a sculptor wants to sculpt, she takes a block of clay and carves away anything that isn't a horse or a castle or a bust of Rodney Dangerfield or whatever she's trying to sculpt. But the writer has an extra step: she must create the block of clay *first*, which is the rough draft, and *then* go back and carve away until she comes up with something to be proud of.

If you only submit the first draft of your writing, essentially all you're doing is giving your reader a giant block of clay.

CHAPTER 30

Presentation

When I started teaching full time in 1992, the essays I assigned always came in as handwritten papers. This was years before personal computers were widely used, and we typically required our students give us their rough drafts (our equivalent of the math department's "show your work" dictum). Still, handwritten essays were the norm.

The first baby that was thrown out with the bathwater was cursive. My wise department chairperson, who had been in the classroom for over thirty years at that point, said she'd been doing a great deal of research and there was no indication that a paper written by a student in cursive was any better or worse than one where the student had printed. So we started making print an option, and many students snapped it up immediately.

As the years passed and computers became more ubiquitous, we began to give extra credit to those students who could provide a typed copy of their essays. It was always a blessed relief when I flipped to the next paper and saw a typed essay. I was less than ten years into my teaching career when it became required for students to type their papers because of the proliferation of laptops, Chromebook carts, and home computers and printers. After that, we never looked back. In fact, it's a mystery to me how, for so many years, I was able to make it through those handwritten papers at all.

Why do typed papers make such a difference?

Because presentation matters.

Business coach Courtney Foster-Donahue teaches others how to create passive income by producing and marketing online courses. She even taught me how to make a few of my own. During my training, she often talked about the importance of presentation when you're giving your audience something new. She used the metaphor of a present. "If you're giving someone a Christmas or birthday present," she would say, "you wouldn't just hand them whatever you bought them and say, 'Here you go' and walk away. Of course not! What you would do is wrap it up in pretty wrapping paper, put a nice big bow on it, and then present it to them with a smile. In addition to *what* you gave them, you would want them to like *how* you gave it to them as well. That's part of the fun. In fact, it may even be at a party. In other words, you make it an event—something to get excited about."

Teachers know this as well. While you can just plunk a worksheet down in front of a student and say, "Good luck, sailor!" you will have much more success—and it will be much more fun for you as the teacher—if you present it in a way that excites and engages your students.

In other words, for your writing to be well-received, you must package it.

In writing, presentation means that the assignment, manuscript, or document you are submitting looks the best it can possibly look. It means that you've shown tremendous care and effort in how it's put together. It means you've taken time with the aesthetics, following the conventions and etiquette of submitting. The last thing you want is for the teacher (or publisher) to be annoyed before he or she even reads a word of what you've written, am I right?

I tell my students that if a teacher is looking at their papers and the font is too small, it's not double-spaced, the spacing is off, or the paragraph indentation is weird, most likely the teacher is already annoyed, and if the teacher is annoyed before she even begins to read the paper, the overall assessment is not going to go the way you want it to.

For the sake of argument, let's assume that we're talking about your typical high school multi-paragraph essay—a classic I assume most of you reading this still assign on the regular.

In that case, "good" presentation typically looks like this:

- **The document is double-spaced.** The old-fashioned reason for this is because the extra space allowed editors to get their red pens in between lines to edit and make notes.
- **12-point font.** The document should be in 12-point font. As I tell my students, 10-point is too small (my eyes!), and 14-point is too big (what is this goofy clown essay I see before me?). The Goldilocks-style "just right" standard of perfect and maximum font-osity is 12-point.
- **Format.** The writer has used MLA, APA, or *Chicago Manual of Style* formatting, especially if they're citing sources. Which one they use depends on what their teacher and school prefer. As I always tell my private tutoring clients, "The number one rule is to always do what your teacher says. Even if it conflicts with what I tell you."
- **No wacky fonts.** If the font is too ornate, I'm going to laugh at the essay, and this is not the reaction the student is shooting for.

Are there other rules, specifications, and guidelines for turning in work? Of course. But if the student has all the aforementioned elements in place before the teacher even begins reading the work, then they will silently and subconsciously thank the writer for going easy on their eyes, and the outcome—a high grade or publication or whatever the carrot on the stick is—will be much better.

And if, as a writer yourself, you send out your own work, it is critical that you follow submission guidelines and specifications as outlined by the publisher, literary agent, or independent literary journal to which you are entrusting your words.

I remember, for example, that when I was submitting poetry and short stories to literary journals in the eighties and nineties, most journals had a very strict rule against simultaneous submissions. For the uninitiated, this means that if you sent your story "Brad Pitt's Left Eyebrow" to the *New Yorker*, it was verboten to send that same story to the *Atlantic Monthly* until you received a response from the *New Yorker*. Each publication presumably wanted first right of refusal and to know that you had chosen them as your one and only (right up until they said "no thank you," that is).

If you chose to disregard that rule and were discovered, not only would you likely get a bad reputation with those particular editors, but if the universe smiled on you and you received an acceptance letter, you would have to contact the other publisher to withdraw your piece from consideration. The problem with this restriction, of course, is that writers, because they are actual human beings, generally only live eighty or ninety years, and when it can take as long as six months to a year to receive a response, they might find themselves in the local old folks' home before they're able to submit something to another publication.

Did writers still mail off simultaneous submissions?

Did I?

Of course.

But much like the student who doesn't double-space his or her essay or use the proper font in an assignment, it always came with certain risks, potential consequences, and moments of gut-twisting anxiety.

So when writing, make sure you follow the rules. At least until you don't follow the rules in a way that makes you the new Jay McInerney or Donald Barthelme. And then, when submitting those wacky, experimental stories, make sure you follow the rules again.

CHAPTER 31

Gestation

There is a strange limbo in the writing process where you are between projects. I'm sure most students don't give it a second thought, other than offering a merciful prayer to the heavens that the next essay is far off on the horizon.

But some writers—maybe those like me, for whom writing is a compulsion—may panic, feeling that the well has gone dry, that there is nothing else to say, that they may never commit another word to paper as long as they live. They may feel lost, restless, or uneasy. They sometimes experience malaise or confusion, unsure of the next step.

You might also experience a time of unease, of grieving the loss of the project that has given your artistic pursuits a definitive purpose for the last few weeks, months, or even years. No matter how you feel regarding moving forward with your writing practice, know that it is all normal and simply a season of your creative life. This, too, shall pass, and you will move on to a new project soon enough.

In fact, if writing truly is a continuum, this potential panic and uncertainty can be easily assuaged. You realize that being between projects is the way of things. You understand that, if you're patient, more words will come. You embrace the mindfulness of things being how they are and knowing that they are as they should be.

In artistic circles, this limbo is often referred to as "gestation."

Gestation is a when things are being allowed to incubate, to grow, even to "cook" a bit. It can be a period of recharging, of refilling the tank. But you can imagine how, if you've ever heard that old cliché that "writers write," this period of downtime may be particularly uncomfortable to the wordsmiths in your life.

In an article, author, artist, and all-around-creative-type Austin Kleon quotes bell hooks as saying, "Whenever I finish a work, I always feel lost, as though a steady anchor has been taken away and there is no sure ground under my feet. During the time between ending one project and beginning another, I always have a crisis of meaning. I begin to wonder what my life is all about and what I have been put on this earth to do. It is as though immersed in a project I lose all sense of myself and must then, when the work is done, rediscover who I am and where I am going."

hooks describes that unpleasant feeling of feeling adrift after you finish a piece of writing and you aren't sure where to turn. And if you identify as a writer, the gestation period can be accompanied by a lost sense of purpose and identity. The world can feel unstable, and your creative impulse and output can seem unpredictable.

But do not fear.

Gestation can also be a beautiful, rich, and empowering period of growth.

Allowing your creative juices to percolate can also take many forms. Gestation can look like:

- reading, especially poetry,
- looking at art,
- painting,
- working jigsaw puzzles,
- or producing a podcast.

One of my favorite places in San Diego, for example, is Balboa Park. Adjacent to downtown San Diego, it is a huge park that contains a multitude of art, science, and history museums, a Spanish-themed art village with working artists, beautiful architecture, breathtaking gardens, and winding hiking paths. It's almost always calm and tranquil. As a bonus, it is right next door to world-famous San Diego Zoo. Balboa Park is one of my go-to places when my soul needs a tune-up, a favorite place to recharge my battery, refill my tank, and renew my spirit. I always feel more refreshed and creative after a few hours in the park. In fact, in anticipation of that, I often bring my camera with me and snap some photos while I'm there.

I also generally bring a journal with me on these sojourns. Not because I am actively working on a piece of writing (though I may be), but because it's possible that by filling my tank I may get random and serendipitous ideas that I am interested in capturing, and so I want to make sure I have the means to jot them down. Regardless of your approach, gestation is nothing to fear or avoid. It is a necessary part of the writing process that, ultimately, leads you to the next project.

Think of it this way: if the car is out of gas, it's not going to run, and you're not going to get anywhere. To use another analogy, sometimes fields must be fallow for a season so that growing and harvesting a bountiful crop the following season is possible.

Think of your subconscious as the field and your craft as the crop.

Therefore, it is important to let the field breathe before you plant more seeds.

That's why I don't worry anymore. I know that there will be periods of time when I am not writing and, very possibly, when I am not even *thinking* about writing.

Similarly, when I start to feel restless and start thinking in language and words and imagery and details, and I think maybe it's time to start putting words on paper again . . .

I listen to that, too.

The key to embracing gestation is to be okay with it, welcome it, know that it is a normal part of the dance, a necessary part of the choreography.

Making sure you cultivate time and space for gestation is crucial. The beauty part is that it helps us learn to trust the process, our intuition, our intelligence, and our craft.

Danny's Writing Diary:

For the Teacher's Soul

About ten years ago, a former student of mine, Monica P., asked if she could stop by my classroom. She said she had something she wanted to give me. I said of course.

Monica was bright, inquisitive, and kind. She was one of those dream students that every teacher sometimes has. Her work ethic was stellar, and she was always one of the best writers in her class. Almost without exception, reading her essays was a joy, not a chore. So I was happy to have her come by, see her again, and get an update on her life.

On the day she came to visit, she and I spent several minutes sharing details of our lives and catching up. Eventually, though, she reached into her bag and pulled out a book.

The branding on the cover of the book was instantly recognizable. It was one of Jack Canfield and Mark Victor Hansen's Chicken Soup for the Soul books. My first, rather selfish, thought was "How nice. She remembered me fondly as a teacher and is going to give me a gift."

I was partly right.

She did gift me the book, which was called Chicken Soup for the Soul: Tough Times for Teens: 101 Stories about the Hardest Parts of Being a Teenager, *but it was her explanation of why she was giving it to me that blew my mind.*

"I wanted to show this to you, Mr. T.," she said. "Look on page 37."

When I looked on page 37, I saw an essay called "She Was Full of Dreams."

Then I looked at the author's name.

"Monica?" I said, stunned. "You wrote this?"

"Yes," she said. "I wanted to give you a copy of this book, not only because I was published in it but because that essay started as an assignment in your class."

Seeing Monica's essay in that edition of Canfield's extraordinarily popular series was one of the watershed moments of my teaching career. It was both personally and professionally fulfilling. It's hard to articulate what it means knowing that the piece she wrote originated in my class. I will always be indebted to Monica for sharing that with me.

To her credit as a smart, hardworking, creative individual with a killer writing style, she went on to graduate from college with a degree in communications and became a very successful on-camera news anchor and news producer in Northern California.

We've kept in touch, and I have also learned from her as I built my own business as an author and entrepreneur and have asked her for advice and guidance on how to pursue media outlets for more publicity. We have come full circle, and the teacher has become the student.

One more instance of yin-yang.

It is always a joy to help my students write, but to be a part of the process of their getting published in such a meaningful way is more profoundly fulfilling than I could have ever imagined.

Such a blessing.

Final Draft Assignments

1. Have your students review and refine their presentation. Explain that the better their paper looks and the easier it is to read, the more favorably you'll be looking at it.

2. If you are submitting your writing (a poem, a book, a grant proposal, whatever), review all submission guidelines and make sure you are following each one as accurately as possible.

3. Don't spill coffee on it. Like I did on an early version of this manuscript.

CONCLUSION

Start a New Path

Life is often about starting new paths. Whether it's a positive change, such as marriage, college graduation, or a new job, or a more trying transition such as divorce, the death of a loved one, or illness, our journey on this planet often entails moving in a new direction. Sometimes even if we are resistant. Sometimes even if we don't particularly want to.

But being a mindful person means understanding that everything is as it should be, and if I want things to be different, it's up to me to make different choices. Once, as I was in a courtroom in downtown San Diego filing my own divorce papers, I saw a sign on a bulletin board: "Nothing changes if nothing changes."

Words to live by.

Our paths may diverge from time to time, but they are always our paths, and we do have influence over where we're headed.

Writing is no different.

After you have finished a piece of writing, gotten feedback, revised it until it shines, sent it off into the world, and then spent some time in gestation, focusing on other pursuits so that you can refill the cup, it's time to start something new.

That "something new" might be a poem, a story, an essay, or even a novel.

It will be whatever you're inspired to create.

What method you choose doesn't matter.

If you hear nothing else in this book, hear this: Writing is about process, about expression, about understanding, about communication. It is a continuum, and it is never about a single piece.

The amazing (and sometimes frustrating) dynamic in writing is that with each new project, you are starting all over again at the beginning. Each new piece has its own purpose and audience. You can't just do the same thing you did last time. That's both a curse and a cause for celebration. While it can increase anxiety—for you and your students ("We have to do *another* essay? We just *did* one!")—it's also exhilarating to know that I am not bound by the mistakes I made the last time I was in front of the keyboard or when my pen was last poised over my journal.

When you start that new writing path, you have some questions to ask yourself.

- What will I be writing? What form will it take?
- Who will be reading it?
- What am I trying to say?
- How will I share it?

But you might be thinking, "What if my path doesn't look like anyone else's?"

No matter.

No one else will have your path. Your path is like your fingerprint.

Starting a new path can be scary and unsettling. It can seem new and uncertain.

That's when you trust in the process.

That's when you say to yourself, "I've stared down a blank sheet of paper before and made it happen. I've put the black squiggles on the white page many times. I've got this."

Counterculture psychologist, philosopher, and author Ram Dass, who wrote the mindfulness classic *Be Here Now*, once said, "Don't compare your path with anybody else's. Your path is unique to you."

That's when you remind yourself that writing is a gift you give yourself not because you love the result or destination, but because you love the doing of it. You love pushing nouns against verbs. You love the rhythm and music of language. You love sharing your ideas and learning from your own expression.

Your writing path is an exhilarating, challenging, and unique expression of your passions, desire, and identity.

Own it. Express it. Have faith in it.

The words you and your students commit to paper will save you.

About the Author

Dan Tricarico has been a high school English teacher for over thirty years. He is also the author of *The Zen Teacher: Creating Focus, Simplicity, and Tranquility in the Classroom* and *Sanctuaries: Self-Care Secrets for Stressed Out Teachers*. In his spare time, he enjoys writing, listening to music, reading mystery novels, watching movies, and staring out of windows. One of his first loves is writing poetry, and he has published many poems both in print and online.

Let Dan Tricarico Help Your Staff

Book Dan for a workshop that shows your staff how to sharpen their skills and improve their lives!

Current workshops/keynotes include:

1. **The Zen Teacher Retreat:** Dan helps your staff learn to reduce their stress, improve their self-care, and avoid burnout using his proprietary Five-Step Zen Teacher Blueprint. This workshop shows teachers how to maximize their performance without sacrificing themselves.

2. **Write Here and Now: The Mindful Writing Teacher's Plan for Finding the Zen in Their Pen:** Dan shows you how to use mindfulness as a secret weapon. This workshop includes tools and strategies from this book that increase participants' ease in their writing process and allow them to find more joy in their writing practice.

Let Dan teach your staff the tools and strategies that will make teaching easier. Educators around the country have benefited from his workshops and have implemented the many approaches he shares in his fun, engaging, interactive workshops.

To request a quote for a workshop, send an email to Dan at **teachingzen@gmail.com**, or fill out the workshop contact form at **thezenteacher.com**.

References

"61 Ram Dass Quotes—Wisdom from a Spiritual Master." *Uganda Empya*, August 27, 2022. https://www.ugandaempya.com/ram-dass-quotes/.

Atlas, Nava. "Quotes by Isak Dinesen on Life and Storytelling." *Literary Ladies Guide*, updated December 29, 2020. https://www.literaryladiesguide.com/author-quotes/isak-dinesen-quotes/.

Babauta, Leo. "Approaching Life with Beginner's Mind." *Zen Habits*, April 21, 2022. https://zenhabits.net/beginner/.

Bainton, George. *The Art of Authorship: Literary Reminiscences, Methods of Work, and Advice to Young Beginners*. New York: D. Appleton, 1891.

Bunting, Joe. "7 Words to Avoid in Writing to Be a Better Writer." *The Write Practice*, April 30, 2021. https://thewritepractice.com/better-writer-now/.

Chödrön, Pema. *When Things Fall Apart: Heart Advice for Difficult Times*. Boston: Shambhala, 1997.

Cotter, Holland. "On Sontag: Essayist as Metaphor and Muse," *New York Times*, August 18, 2006. https://www.nytimes.com/2006/08/18/arts/design/18sont.html.

Csikszentmihalyi, Mihaly. *Flow: The Psychology of Optimal Experience*. New York: Harper and Row, 2009.

Deresiewicz, William. "First Thought, Best Thought," *New York Times*, April 8, 2001. https://archive.nytimes.com/www.nytimes.com/

books/01/04/08/reviews/010408.08deresit.html?source=post_page---------------------------.

Douglas, Blake. "Heraclitus." *Enotes.com*, February 4, 2020. https://www.enotes.com/homework-help/heraclitus-said-you-cannot-step-into-the-same-377647.

"Elmore Leonard: 10 Rules for Good Writing." *Gotham Writers Workshop*. https://www.writingclasses.com/toolbox/tips-masters/elmore-leonard-10-rules-for-good-writing.

Gladwell, Malcolm. *David and Goliath: Underdogs, Misfits, and the Art of Battling Giants*. New York: Little Brown, 2013.

Godin, Seth. "The Simple Cure for Writer's Block." *Seth's Blog*, June 30, 2020. https://seths.blog/2020/06/the-simple-cure-for-writers-block/.

Goldberg, Natalie. "The Rules for Writing Practice." https://writ101van.weebly.com/uploads/2/2/7/3/22735066/goldberg_rules_of_writing_practice_text.pdf.

Goldberg, Natalie. *Wild Mind: Living the Writers Life*. New York: Bantam, 1990.

Goldberg, Natalie. *Writing Down the Bones: Freeing the Writer Within*. Boston: Shambhala, 1986.

Grove, Nancy. "E. L. Doctorow in Quotes: 15 of His Best." *The Guardian*, July 21, 2015. https://www.theguardian.com/books/2015/jul/22/el-doctorow-in-quotes-15-of-his-best.

Hemingway, Ernest. *Death in the Afternoon*. New York: Scribner, 2015.

Herrigel, Eugen. *Zen and the Art of Archery*. New York: Vintage, 1971.

"Journaling as Meditation." *Mind Fuel Daily*, May 20, 2018. https://www.mindfueldaily.com/livewell/journaling-as-mediation/.

Julia Cameron Live. "Morning Pages." https://juliacameronlive.com/basic-tools/morning-pages/.

Kleon, Austin. "Teach Your Tongue to Say I Don't Know." *Austin Kleon* (blog), November 9, 2019. https://austinkleon.com/2019/11/09/teach-your-tongue-to-say-i-dont-know/.

Kleon, Austin. "What's Next?" *Austin Kleon* (blog), May 14, 2018. https://austinkleon.com/2018/05/14/whats-next/.

Lamott, Anne. *Bird by Bird*. New York: Anchor Books, 1994.

"Malcom Gladwell Teaches Writing." *MasterClass Online Classes*. https://www.masterclass.com/classes/malcolm-gladwell-teaches-writing.

Oliver, Mary. "Yes! No!" https://www.poetry-chaikhana.com/Poets/O/OliverMary/YesNo/index.html.

Poetry Foundation. "Ernest M. Hemingway." https://www.poetryfoundation.org/poets/ernest-m-hemingway.

Sontag, Susan. "A Writer, I Think, Is Someone Who Pays Attention to the World." *Quotes of Famous People*, updated June 9, 2022. https://quotepark.com/quotes/840304-susan-sontag-a-writer-i-think-is-someone-who-pays-attention-t/.

"Sweet Brown: Ain't Nobody Got Time for That (Autotune Remix)." The Parody Factory, dir. *YouTube*, April 14, 2012. https://www.youtube.com/watch?v=bFEoMO0pc7k.

Zielin, Lara. "Happe." https://www.lara-zielin.com/happe.

Acknowledgments

I am greatly indebted to the following people, who have improved the quality of my teaching, my writing, and/or my life.

Thanks to my publishers at DBC, Inc., Dave and Shelley Burgess, who continue changing my life for the better.

Thanks to Lindsey Alexander, Salvatore Borriello, Sara Jaffe, Liz Schreiter, and the rest of the team at the Reading List.

Thanks, gratitude, and love to my parents, Michael and Janet Tricarico, who gave me life and then always encouraged me to make the most of it and do whatever I wanted it with it. I've tried to honor that always.

Thanks, gratitude, and all my love to the two best daughters I could have hoped for: Tatum Ann and Tessa Marie, who constantly inspire me to be a better father and a more decent person.

I would also like to express much thanks and gratitude to:

The West Hills High School English department, especially those who have gone on to other adventures—namely Jane Schaffer, Anne Foster, Kristin McLaughlin, and John Holler.

The Zen Teacher Inner Circle: Melody McAllister, Theresa Holloran, Jamie Leach, Jaime Bart, Angela Watson, Anna Marie Savino, Akilah Ellison, Dallas Koehn, Brenda Cavin Grizzle, Lloyd Day, and Margaret Dowling Murphy. Thank you for believing in me and my message.

The Prime 2 Shine Super Stars: Krista Leh, Tammy Musiowsky-Borneman, Robert Abney, Elisabeth Bostwick, Cathy Trimble, Michelle Griffin, Samantha Mullins, Vicki Miller, Julia Skolnik, and Mercedeh Kermanshahi, LaRae Locker Whitely, Lisa Knee Gaede, Erin Kiger, Vicki Martin Wilson, Elizabeth Kennedy Merce, Liesl Sisson, Naomi

Church, Dr. Maribeth Edmunds, Jodi Moskowitz, Cheri Dotterer, Jamie Davis, Krista Kulp Venza, and Brady Liming.

The Business Guides: LaVonna Roth, Beth Perry, Chris Winfield, Jen Gottlieb, Jamie DuBose, Todd Herman, and the best business muse in town, Courtney Foster-Donahue.

The Teachers: Terry Theroux, Paula Skrifvars, Robin Luby, Kay Adams, Geoffrey Anderson, Suzanne Geba, Danelle Barton, Chris Morrissey, and Sandy LaPlant.

The Friends: Laura Preble, Lara Zielin, Heather Ophir, Jeff and DeAnna Thill, Judy Hill Gagne, and Teresa and Joe Shea.

And finally, to Chrissy.

This one's for you . . . out loud.

More from Dave Burgess Consulting, Inc.

Since 2012, DBCI has published books that inspire and equip educators to be their best. For more information on our titles or to purchase bulk orders for your school, district, or book study, visit **DaveBurgessConsulting.com/DBCIbooks**.

Like a PIRATE™ Series

Teach Like a PIRATE by Dave Burgess
eXPlore Like a PIRATE by Michael Matera
Learn Like a PIRATE by Paul Solarz
Plan Like a PIRATE by Dawn M. Harris
Play Like a PIRATE by Quinn Rollins
Run Like a PIRATE by Adam Welcome
Tech Like a PIRATE by Matt Miller

Lead Like a PIRATE™ Series

Lead Like a PIRATE by Shelley Burgess and Beth Houf
Balance Like a PIRATE by Jessica Cabeen, Jessica Johnson, and Sarah Johnson
Lead beyond Your Title by Nili Bartley
Lead with Appreciation by Amber Teamann and Melinda Miller
Lead with Culture by Jay Billy
Lead with Instructional Rounds by Vicki Wilson
Lead with Literacy by Mandy Ellis
She Leads by Dr. Rachael George and Majalise W. Tolan

Leadership & School Culture

Beyond the Surface of Restorative Practices by Marisol Rerucha
Change the Narrative by Henry J. Turner and Kathy Lopes
Choosing to See by Pamela Seda and Kyndall Brown
Culturize by Jimmy Casas
Discipline Win by Andy Jacks
Escaping the School Leader's Dunk Tank by Rebecca Coda and Rick Jetter
Fight Song by Kim Bearden
From Teacher to Leader by Starr Sackstein
If the Dance Floor Is Empty, Change the Song by Joe Clark
The Innovator's Mindset by George Couros
It's OK to Say "They" by Christy Whittlesey
Kids Deserve It! by Todd Nesloney and Adam Welcome
Leading the Whole Teacher by Allyson Apsey
Let Them Speak by Rebecca Coda and Rick Jetter
The Limitless School by Abe Hege and Adam Dovico
Live Your Excellence by Jimmy Casas
Next-Level Teaching by Jonathan Alsheimer
The Pepper Effect by Sean Gaillard
Principaled by Kate Barker, Kourtney Ferrua, and Rachael George
The Principled Principal by Jeffrey Zoul and Anthony McConnell
Relentless by Hamish Brewer
The Secret Solution by Todd Whitaker, Sam Miller, and Ryan Donlan
Start. Right. Now. by Todd Whitaker, Jeffrey Zoul, and Jimmy Casas
Stop. Right. Now. by Jimmy Casas and Jeffrey Zoul
Teachers Deserve It by Rae Hughart and Adam Welcome
Teach Your Class Off by CJ Reynolds
They Call Me "Mr. De" by Frank DeAngelis
Thrive through the Five by Jill M. Siler
Unmapped Potential by Julie Hasson and Missy Lennard
When Kids Lead by Todd Nesloney and Adam Dovico
Word Shift by Joy Kirr

Your School Rocks by Ryan McLane and Eric Lowe

Technology & Tools

50 Things to Go Further with Google Classroom by Alice Keeler and Libbi Miller

50 Things You Can Do with Google Classroom by Alice Keeler and Libbi Miller

140 Twitter Tips for Educators by Brad Currie, Billy Krakower, and Scott Rocco

Block Breaker by Brian Aspinall

Building Blocks for Tiny Techies by Jamila "Mia" Leonard

Code Breaker by Brian Aspinall

The Complete EdTech Coach by Katherine Goyette and Adam Juarez

Control Alt Achieve by Eric Curts

The Esports Education Playbook by Chris Aviles, Steve Isaacs, Christine Lion-Bailey, and Jesse Lubinsky

Google Apps for Littles by Christine Pinto and Alice Keeler

Master the Media by Julie Smith

Raising Digital Leaders by Jennifer Casa-Todd

Reality Bytes by Christine Lion-Bailey, Jesse Lubinsky, and Micah Shippee, PhD

Sail the 7 Cs with Microsoft Education by Becky Keene and Kathi Kersznowski

Shake Up Learning by Kasey Bell

Social LEADia by Jennifer Casa-Todd

Stepping Up to Google Classroom by Alice Keeler and Kimberly Mattina

Teaching Math with Google Apps by Alice Keeler and Diana Herrington

Teachingland by Amanda Fox and Mary Ellen Weeks

Teaching with Google Jamboard by Alice Keeler and Kimberly Mattina

Teaching Methods & Materials

All 4s and 5s by Andrew Sharos
Boredom Busters by Katie Powell
The Classroom Chef by John Stevens and Matt Vaudrey
The Collaborative Classroom by Trevor Muir
Copyrighteous by Diana Gill
CREATE by Bethany J. Petty
Deploying EduProtocols by Kim Voge, with Jon Corippo and Marlena Hebern
Ditch That Homework by Matt Miller and Alice Keeler
Ditch That Textbook by Matt Miller
Don't Ditch That Tech by Matt Miller, Nate Ridgway, and Angelia Ridgway
EDrenaline Rush by John Meehan
Educated by Design by Michael Cohen, The Tech Rabbi
The EduProtocol Field Guide by Marlena Hebern and Jon Corippo
The EduProtocol Field Guide: Book 2 by Marlena Hebern and Jon Corippo
The EduProtocol Field Guide: Math Edition by Lisa Nowakowski and Jeremiah Ruesch
The EduProtocol Field Guide: Social Studies Edition by Dr. Scott M. Petri and Adam Moler
Empowered to Choose: A Practical Guide to Personalized Learning by Andrew Easton
Expedition Science by Becky Schnekser
Frustration Busters by Katie Powell
Fully Engaged by Michael Matera and John Meehan
Game On? Brain On! by Lindsay Portnoy, PhD
Guided Math AMPED by Reagan Tunstall
Innovating Play by Jessica LaBar-Twomy and Christine Pinto
Instructional Coaching Connection by Nathan Lang-Raad
Instant Relevance by Denis Sheeran

Keeping the Wonder by Jenna Copper, Ashley Bible, Abby Gross, and Staci Lamb
LAUNCH by John Spencer and A.J. Juliani
Learning in the Zone by Dr. Sonny Magana
Lights, Cameras, TEACH! by Kevin J. Butler
Make Learning MAGICAL by Tisha Richmond
Pass the Baton by Kathryn Finch and Theresa Hoover
Project-Based Learning Anywhere by Lori Elliott
Pure Genius by Don Wettrick
The Revolution by Darren Ellwein and Derek McCoy
Shift This! by Joy Kirr
Skyrocket Your Teacher Coaching by Michael Cary Sonbert
Spark Learning by Ramsey Musallam
Sparks in the Dark by Travis Crowder and Todd Nesloney
Table Talk Math by John Stevens
Unpack Your Impact by Naomi O'Brien and LaNesha Tabb
The Wild Card by Hope and Wade King
Writefully Empowered by Jacob Chastain
The Writing on the Classroom Wall by Steve Wyborney
You Are Poetry by Mike Johnston

Inspiration, Professional Growth & Personal Development

Be REAL by Tara Martin
Be the One for Kids by Ryan Sheehy
The Coach ADVenture by Amy Illingworth
Creatively Productive by Lisa Johnson
Educational Eye Exam by Alicia Ray
The EduNinja Mindset by Jennifer Burdis
Empower Our Girls by Lynmara Colón and Adam Welcome
Finding Lifelines by Andrew Grieve and Andrew Sharos
The Four O'Clock Faculty by Rich Czyz
How Much Water Do We Have? by Pete and Kris Nunweiler
P Is for Pirate by Dave and Shelley Burgess

A Passion for Kindness by Tamara Letter
The Path to Serendipity by Allyson Apsey
Rogue Leader by Rich Czyz
Sanctuaries by Dan Tricarico
Saving Sycamore by Molly B. Hudgens
The SECRET SAUCE by Rich Czyz
Shattering the Perfect Teacher Myth by Aaron Hogan
Stories from Webb by Todd Nesloney
Talk to Me by Kim Bearden
Teach Better by Chad Ostrowski, Tiffany Ott, Rae Hughart, and Jeff Gargas
Teach Me, Teacher by Jacob Chastain
Teach, Play, Learn! by Adam Peterson
The Teachers of Oz by Herbie Raad and Nathan Lang-Raad
TeamMakers by Laura Robb and Evan Robb
Through the Lens of Serendipity by Allyson Apsey
The Zen Teacher by Dan Tricarico

Children's Books

Alpert by LaNesha Tabb
Alpert & Friends by LaNesha Tabb
Beyond Us by Aaron Polansky
Cannonball In by Tara Martin
Dolphins in Trees by Aaron Polansky
I Can Achieve Anything by MoNique Waters
I Want to Be a Lot by Ashley Savage
Micah's Big Question by Naomi O'Brien
The Princes of Serendip by Allyson Apsey
Ride with Emilio by Richard Nares
A Teacher's Top Secret Confidential by LaNesha Tabb
A Teacher's Top Secret: Mission Accomplished by LaNesha Tabb
The Wild Card Kids by Hope and Wade King
Zom-Be a Design Thinker by Amanda Fox

Made in the USA
Las Vegas, NV
26 October 2022